ARTS & CRAFTS FURNITURE

MARK F. MORAN

Identification and Price Guide

©2004 Krause Publication
Published by

krause publications
An imprint of F+W Publications, Inc.

700 East State Street • Iola, WI 54990-0001
715-445-2214 • 888-457-2873
www.krause.com

Our toll-free number to place an order or obtain
a free catalog is (800) 258-0929.

Library of Congress Catalog Number: 2004093890

ISBN: 0-87349-815-1

Edited by Dennis Thornton
Designed by Jamie Griffin

Printed in China

WARMAN'S ARTS & CRAFTS FURNITURE

✎ LESS IS MORE ✎

Collectors of Arts & Crafts furniture and accessories have had the same rallying cry for the last 100 years: "Less is more!"

What drives the market today is the ongoing research into design details and construction techniques that helps to distinguish the generic mission-style furniture from the work of the masters, who we'll discuss shortly.

In his 1908 essay titled, "Ornament and Crime," the Austrian architect Adolf Loos wrote: "The evolution of culture is synonymous with the removal of ornament from utilitarian objects."

Arts & Crafts devotees would agree. This design movement was a reaction to the excesses of the Victorian era when an unadorned surface was considered incomplete.

Loos pulled no punches in his attacks on the then-contemporary style, using a phrase that would be echoed in the 1984 Wendy's commercial that made Clara Peller a star:

"The advocate of ornament believes that my urge for simplicity is in the nature of a mortification. No, respected professor at the school of applied art, I am not mortifying myself! The dishes of past centuries, which display all kinds of ornaments to make peacocks, pheasants, and lobsters look more tasty, have exactly the opposite effect on me. I am horrified when I go through a cookery exhibition and think that I am meant to eat these stuffed carcasses. I eat roast beef!"

In his essay, Loos railed not only against the taste for the overly ornamented, but also against what he believed were misguided attempts to adapt ornament to fit the times, as in art nouveau.

"Ornament is not only produced by criminals; it itself commits a crime, by damaging men's health, the national economy and cultural development. Ornament is no longer a natural product of our civilization, it accordingly represents backwardness or degeneration.

"No one can create ornament now who lives on our level of culture."

Nevertheless, the Arts & Crafts movement absorbed the design themes of art nouveau, Chinese and Japanese aesthetics, and American innovation to create an enduring style.

On the cover:
Gustav Stickley desk/bookcase
designed by Harvey Ellis, with a drop-front desk over two drawers and flanked by two bookcase doors with leaded glass panels, iron hardware. Original finish with original interior, including inkwells, intact, minor chip to top, a few chips repaired. Probably purchased from Gustav Stickley in 1903. 56" by 56" by 15"

$100,000+

✐ ARTS & CRAFTS HISTORY IN BRIEF ✐

The design movement that came to be called Arts & Crafts had its beginnings in the social commentaries of the British scholar and critic John Ruskin (1819-1900).

Ruskin rejected the concept of machine-made products, calling them "dishonest." He believed that craftsmanship wrought by hand brought dignity to labor, and he founded a utopian Arts & Crafts community in 1871.

A British contemporary of Ruskin was designer William Morris (1834-1896), whose legacy is preserved in the solid and sturdy armchairs that bear his name.

In 1897, a group of Vienna artists and innovators left the established Künstlerhaus and became known as the Vienna Secession. Their goals included cultural exchanges with other European artists, and they embraced the design trends based on the Arts & Crafts philosophy and the French art nouveau style.

This led to the formation of the Wiener Werkstätte (Vienna Workshop) in 1903, founded on the concept of "Gesamtkunstwerk" (total artwork), a term originated by composer Richard Wagner, in which all the individual arts would contribute under the direction of a single creative mind in order to express one overriding idea.

While the Wiener Werkstätte was inspired by Ruskin and Morris, it was also based on the British Guild and School of Handicraft founded by architect Charles Robert Ashbee (1863-1942). Although Ashbee was influenced by the styles of Gothic Revival architecture, he also promoted the work of Frank Lloyd Wright and the American Prairie School.

The Scottish architect and designer, Charles Rennie Mackintosh (1868-1928) helped to meld the art nouveau and Arts & Crafts movements into a distinctive style whose influences spread across Europe, and had a lasting effect on five brothers born in the wilds of Wisconsin.

The eldest, Gustav Stickley, was born on March 9, 1858, in Osceola, Wis. Though he was trained as a stonemason, Stickley learned furniture making at his uncle's chair factory in Pennsylvania.

After a trip to Europe in 1896, he returned to the United States and founded the United Crafts of Eastwood, N.Y. The furniture he designed and made was mostly of American oak. It was of a sturdy and plain design, in contrast to the highly decorated late-Victorian pieces popular at the time. Though this design movement became known as "Mission Style"—after the simple, functional pieces used in Spanish California missions—Stickley never used these words to describe his products.

Tilt-top lamp table
attributed to J.M. Young (Camden, N.Y., 1890-1979), circa 1910-15, oak, original finish, 30" by 35" diameter
$900-$1,200

Working with architect Harvey Ellis, Stickley also designed house plans that later appeared in two books: Craftsman Homes (1909) and More Craftsman Homes (1912). These books illustrated the homes' exteriors, as well as their interiors, and were accompanied by floor plans.

Cheval mirror
attributed to Stickley Bros., circa 1905-12, oak, original finish, glass and hardware. 67 1/2" tall, 27 1/2" wide
$3,500-$3,800

Harvey Ellis was born in Rochester, N.Y., on Oct. 17, 1852. After a stormy youth, during which he was expelled from military school and then shipped off to Europe by his parents, he began studying architecture and design.

In 1877, Harvey and his brother, Charles, established the architectural office of H. & C.S. Ellis in Rochester, N.Y. After some initial success, disagreements with his brother prompted Harvey in 1885 to move to Utica, N.Y., then to St. Paul, Minn. In 1886-87, he was employed as a draftsman by the St. Paul firms of J. Walter Stevens, Mould & McNichol, and Leroy S. Buffington.

Ellis designed houses, churches, and public buildings (though these were seldom built) for Buffington. He returned to Rochester in 1894 and rejoined his brother's firm.

Ellis' appreciation of the Arts & Crafts movement is apparent in the designs he created during this period. He was a founding member and president of the Rochester Arts & Crafts Society. In 1894, he helped organize the Society's first exhibition, which featured Japanese prints and French posters.

In 1903, Ellis moved to Syracuse, N.Y., at the invitation of Gustav Stickley to write for Stickley's magazine, The Craftsman, and contribute designs for furniture. Ellis published several articles that included his designs for Arts & Crafts homes and interiors. Ellis' use of art nouveau curves and inlays brought a considerably lighter style to some of Stickley's furniture.

Though his influence was felt for decades after, Ellis' association with Stickley was all too brief. He died on Jan. 2, 1904, at the age of 52.

All five Stickley siblings had a profound impact on the American Arts & Crafts movement, though they eventually began to compete against one another and undercut each other's businesses.

In 1883, Charles (c. 1865-1928), Albert (1862-1928), and Gustav (d. 1942) started Stickley Brothers, in Binghamton, N.Y. Albert left that firm and established the Stickley Brothers Furniture Co. with brother John George (1871-1921) in Grand Rapids, Mich., in 1891.

In 1902, John George left Stickley Brothers Furniture Co. to open the Onondaga Shops with brother Leopold (1869-1957) in Fayetteville, N.Y., incorporating four years later as L. & J.G. Stickley, Inc.

Another influential furniture maker of the day was the Charles P. Limbert Co. (1894-1944) of Grand Rapids, Mich.

Limbert was born in Lyonsville, Pa., in 1854. The son of a furniture dealer, he worked as a furniture salesman, and in 1894 he started his Grand Rapids firm, making chairs. He also worked as an agent for other furniture makers, and helped to popularize the "rustic" furniture made by Old Hickory of Martinsville, Ind.

Limbert started making "Dutch Arts and Crafts" style furniture and lighting at his Grand Rapids factory in 1902. He was a student of European furniture designs, especially the Secessionist movement.

Of all American Arts & Crafts furniture makers, Limbert was perhaps best known for his use of decorative cutouts, which often took the form of squares, spades, and hearts.

He opened a factory in Holland, Mich., in 1906 where he produced furniture until 1922, when ill health led him to sell his interest in the company. He died at his home outside Grand Rapids in 1923.

Charles Rohlfs (1853-1936) was one of the Arts & Crafts movement's most innovative designers. He did not follow the simple lines that the Stickley brothers used, instead employing a distinctive style that featured carvings and ornamentation that borrowed from Chinese, medieval, and art nouveau influences.

Rohlfs started his career in woodworking in the 1880s in Buffalo, N.Y. He opened his first commercial workshops in 1898, and the Marshall Field's Department Store held an exhibit of his

Lifetime two-door bookcase
circa 1910-15, oak, refinished, original glass and hardware, divided interior with two shelves on each side, overhanging top, made in Grand Rapids, Mich. 46" by 52" by 14"

$2,500-$3,000

work in 1900. In 1902, Rohlfs was made a fellow of the Royal Society of Arts in London, and he was even commissioned to provide a set of chairs for Buckingham Palace.

In the first decade of the 20th century, Arts & Crafts colonies based on the teachings of Ruskin and Morris flourished briefly in America. The Rose Valley Association (1901-1909) in Rose Valley, Pa., was a utopian community near Philadelphia making furniture and pottery.

Byrdcliffe Arts & Crafts Colony (1902-1910) founded by Ralph Radcliffe Whitehead and his wife, Jane Byrd McCall in Woodstock, N.Y., produced furniture, pottery, textiles, and metalwares.

But the most famous of these groups was built around the energetic personality of Elbert Hubbard.

Born in Bloomington, Ill., in 1856, Elbert Hubbard was a consummate salesman. He became a partner in the J.D. Larkin Co. of Buffalo, N.Y., then one of the most successful mail-order houses in the country. Hubbard was responsible for introducing the system of credit and premiums used to sell the firm's soap products.

In 1893, Hubbard sold his interest in the Larkin Company for $75,000 and "retired" at the age of 36.

When he was unable to find a publisher for his writings, Hubbard established the Roycroft Printing Shop at his home in East Aurora, N.Y., in 1895.

The Roycrofters prospered and by 1905 were operating their own factory, blacksmith shop, farm, bank, and later an inn, which still stands. The inn had to be furnished, so Hubbard had local craftsmen make a simple, unadorned line of furniture in the style of Stickley. The furniture became popular with visitors, and many asked how they could buy pieces for their homes. A furniture manufacturing industry was born.

Originally devoted to the making of books in the manner of William Morris, the Roycrofters soon developed a wide range of arts and crafts items for sale, especially hammered metalwares. What they made to furnish and decorate their expanding Roycroft campus was soon being sold by catalog.

The Roycroft community eventually grew to 500 people under Hubbard's guidance.

From 1905 to 1915, Hubbard was a popular author and lecturer in the United States. But the utopian vision was extinguished when Hubbard and his second wife, Alice, died aboard the Lusitania, sunk by a German torpedo in April 1915.

The Community's leadership passed to Elbert's son, Bert, who took the Roycrofters to wider sales distribution. But changing American tastes led to declining sales, and the Roycrofters ceased operations in 1938.

Stickley Bros. Quaint oversized rocker
(No. 604?), circa 1912-15, oak, original finish, metal tag. 36" tall, 33" wide, 33 1/2" deep

$1,800-$2,200

TIPS FOR COLLECTORS

Finish: Simply put, it's everything. Subtle difference in finish can mean the difference of thousands of dollars in value.

Watch for terms like "refinished," "waxed original finish," "overcoated original finish" (stain or varnish has been added to even out appearance), "restored and enhanced original finish," "skinned original finish" (or heavily cleaned, usually accomplished by using an abrasive to take off the top coat), "lightly cleaned original finish," and "partially refinished with color added." Collectors and dealers may use any combination of these terms to describe finish, so be sure to ask about their definitions of surface condition.

In addition, "skinned" can sometimes refer to the application of veneer.

Condition: Look for signs of repair and restoration, including filled screw holes, replaced seat supports, touch-up to minor scratches, replaced hinge pins and escutcheons, splits near tenons, and veneer lifting and chipping.

Gustav Stickley eight-leg sideboard
circa 1901-04, oak, refinished, original hammered-iron strap hinges and pulls, unmarked, 50" tall (after 1904, this form was slightly shorter). 70" wide, 26" deep
$8,500-$9,500

DESIGN TERMS

Collectors of Arts & Crafts furniture will find that certain terms are common to a wide range of pieces. These include:

Apron: the wooden panel that connects the surface and legs of a table or chair.

Buttress: a projecting structure for supporting or giving stability.

Chamfer: a corner or edge that is cut at an angle or beveled.

Clip-corner: a design element where the corners (usually of a tabletop) are cut at right angles, creating a hexagon with four broad sides and four narrow sides.

Corbel: a brace that projects from within a wall and supports a weight, especially one that is stepped upward and outward from a vertical surface.

Escutcheon: a protective or ornamental plate or flange (as around a keyhole).

Fluted: having or marked by tightly spaced grooves.

Gallery: a small ornamental barrier or railing (as along the edge of a table or shelf).

Key: a small piece of wood or metal used as a wedge or for preventing motion between parts.

Ladder-back: a series of horizontal braces in the back of a chair resembling the rungs of a ladder.

Mortise: a hole, groove, or slot into or through which some other part fits or passes, especially a cavity cut into a piece of wood to receive a tenon.

Mullion: a slender vertical member that forms a division between units of a window, door or screen, or is used decoratively.

Overcoat: a covering, usually of satin or varnish, that protects or enhances the original worn surface.

Pilaster: an upright support that is often rectangular and is structurally a pier, but is treated as a column and usually projects a third of its width or less from the wall.

Pyramidal: of or relating to a pyramid form.

Rail: a bar extending from one post or support to another and serving as a guard or barrier.

Repousse: shaped or ornamented with patterns in relief made by hammering or pressing on the reverse side, used especially for metal.

Skinned: the surface has been cleaned or reduced using an abraisive.

Skirt: a part or attachment serving as a rim, border, or edging.

Slat: a thin flat strip, especially of wood or metal, which may be wide or narrow.

Spindle: a turned, decorative piece of wood that also serves as a brace.

Stretcher: a rod or bar extending between two legs of a chair or table.

Tenon: a projecting member in a piece of wood or other material for insertion into a mortise to make a joint.

Toe board: the trim piece, often decorative, closest to the floor and braced between the front legs of a

❧ ARTS & CRAFTS RESOURCES ❧

This book would not have been possible without the resources and generous assistance of the following:

Carol Eppel Antiques
Antiques St. Croix
124 S. Second St.
Stillwater, MN 55082
(651) 351-2888 or (651) 430-0095

Don Johnson, Randy Brolander
American Arts & Crafts Brokers
1365 Midway Parkway
St. Paul, MN 55108
(651) 644-2731
drj747@comcast.com

David Rago Auctions, Inc.
333 North Main Street
Lambertville, NJ 08530
(609) 397-9374
www.ragoarts.com
info@ragoarts.com

Treadway Gallery, Inc.
2029 Madison Road
Cincinnati, Ohio 45208
(513) 321-6742
Fax: (513) 871-7722
www.treadwaygallery.com
info@treadwaygallery.com

John Toomey Gallery
818 North Boulevard
Oak Park, IL 60301
(708) 383-5234
Fax: (708) 383-4828
info@johntoomeygallery.com

**Gustav Stickley
double costumer**
1906, oak, refinished, missing
one set of hooks, 72 1/2" tall,
13" deep

$2,400-$2,600

✑ SELECTED MAKERS' MARKS ✑

Dozens of American Arts & Crafts furniture manufacturers flourished in the first quarter of the 20th century, but only a few achieved wide recognition based on the quality of their products. Here are some of the marks of the most influential designers and manufacturers.

Greene and Greene, Pasadena, Calif. The shop mark of Charles Sumner Greene (1868-1957) and Henry Mather Greene (1870-1954) is a stylized script that forms a single lariat-like enclosure forming the words "Sumner Greene," interspersed with the words "His True Mark" in block letters.

Charles P. Limbert Co., Grand Rapids, Mich. The Limbert mark, either branded or on a paper label, shows a carpenter working at his bench, and the words, "Limbert's Arts Crafts Furniture—Made in Grand Rapids Michigan." After 1906, the mark reads, "Limbert's Arts Crafts Furniture— Trademark—Made in Grand Rapids and Holland." This mark is found in both rectangular and square shapes in advertising of the period.

Charles Rohlfs, Buffalo, N.Y. Though his pieces may be unmarked, Rohlfs' marks include the branded or carved letter "R" inside a buck saw, sometimes with the year of manufacturer, or "CR" with the year.

The Roycrofters, East Aurora, N.Y. Marks include either the carved word "Roycroft," or a brand of a double cross atop a circle that contains the letter "R."

Shop of the Crafters, Cincinnati, Ohio. The Crafters' rectangular paper label featured a flaring lantern trademark and "Shop of the Crafters at Cincinnati—Oscar Onken Co. Sole Owners."

Charles Stickley, Stickley & Brandt Chair Co. Inc., Binghampton, N.Y. Marks include the impressed signature of Charles Stickley, or a rectangular decal (almost a stylized cauldron shape) with "Stickley & Brandt Chair Company—Charles Stickley (in script) Genl. Mgr."

Stickley Brothers Co., Binghampton, N.Y., and Stickley Brothers Inc., Grand Rapids, Mich. Marks include "Made by Stickley Bros. Grand Rapids Mich." in an oval paper label, or a decal or brass tag reading, "Quaint Furniture Stickley Bros. Co. Grand Rapids, Mich.," or the brand "Quaint SB."

Gustav Stickley, The Craftsman Workshops, Binghampton, Eastwood, and Syracuse, N.Y. The Gustav-Craftsman marks incorporated a joiner's compass, Stickley (in script), and the words "Als Ik Kan" (As Best I Can). These emblems—whether branded, in decals of red and black, or printed on paper labels—were sometimes paired with the "Craftsman" trademark, and the design elements varied slightly over the 14-year life of the company.

Tobey Furniture Co., Chicago There are two circular Tobey marks used over a five-year period from 1900-1905. The first has a rustic appearance and reads, "Tobey Hand Made Furniture— Established 1856 Chicago"; the second circular mark, which covers the time that the firm also sold the designs of Gustav Stickley, reads, "The Tobey Furniture Company—Chicago—The New Furniture"; a third mark found on metal tags reads, "Russmore—The Tobey Furniture Company Trademark—Chicago."

L. & J.G. Stickley Furniture Co., Onondaga Shops, Fayetteville, N.Y. Marks included a wooden hand-screw clamp with "L. & J.G. Stickley—Handcraft"; a rectangular decal, "The Onondaga Shops—L. & J.G. Stickley — Fayetteville, N.Y."; a rectangular decal (red and yellow), "The Work of L. & J.G. Stickley"; and the "co-joined" mark which included both the screw clamp and joiner's compass in a circle, and "Stickley Handcraft Craftsman— Syracuse & Fayetteville, N.Y."

ARTS & CRAFTS FURNITURE

Armoires
(Also see Wardrobe)

Arts & Crafts armoire
probably Austrian, arched form with two doors with copper repousse panels, original finish, 48" by 19" by 76"

$900-$1,100

Gustav Stickley armoire
(No. 624) with cornice top, paneled case, single door over lower drawer and interior fitted with open storage cubby and six-over-five drawers. Several filled screw holes. (This form seldom found with intact interior). Refinished. Unmarked. 71 1/2" by 32" by 20 1/2"

$6,500-$7,500

Beds

Arts & Crafts doll furniture
davenport bed, paneled sides with adjustable back that lays flat or upright, original finish. 25" by 12" by 14"

$40-$60

L. & J.G. Stickley bed
similar to No. 84, single bed with five wide slats supported by tall tapered posts, wear to original finish, unsigned, replaced rails. 44" by 54"

$800-$900

L. & J.G. Stickley full-size bed
with raised posts and twelve vertical slats to head- and footboard, complete with side rails. Original finish to part of the bed, repegged. Co-joined label. Headboard: 50" by 57"

$2,300-$2,800

Arts & Crafts daybed
with single broad slat to each side, and red vinyl cushion. Refinished, minor chips, some looseness. 28" by 28" by 78"

$700-$900

Arts & Crafts daybed
attributed to McHugh (McHugh & Co., New York, active from 1884 to 1916), with square pyramidal posts, side and back with three vertical slats, and replaced upholstery. Refinished, replaced seat supports. Unmarked. 27 1/2" by 57" by 25 1/2"

$800-$1,000

Roycroft double bed
headboard and baseboard with vertical slats, on Mackmurdo feet. Excellent original finish and condition. Orb and cross mark. 49" by 55" by 80"

$5,000-$6,000

Mackmurdo Feet

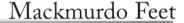

The design term "Mackmurdo feet"—which refers to an abruptly tapering or corseted leg with an angular flared foot—is in tribute to Arthur Heygate Mackmurdo (1851-1942), a disciple of John Ruskin and William Morris. In 1882, Mackmurdo founded the Century Guild in England, to produce work with Arts & Crafts designs.

Gustav Stickley knock-down bed
1902-03, with vertical slats. Minor touch-ups to original finish, finish added to side of posts, overall excellent condition. Stickley box decal, paper label. Both head and foot: 34" by 54" by 84"

$5,000-$6,000

Gustav Stickley single bed
with pyramidal posts, nine spindles to the head- and footboard, complete with side rails. Branded Stickley. 49 1/4" by 43 3/4" by 79 1/2"

$1,000-$1,400

Gustav Stickley oversized twin bed
with four broad vertical slats to head- and footboard, and tapering rabbit-ear posts. Waxed original finish, good condition. Red decal. 46 3/4" by 46 1/2" by 78 1/2"

$1,600-$2,000

Gustav Stickley single bed
with arched top rail and three broad vertical slats to the head- and footboard, complete with broad side rails. Refinished. Red decal. Headboard: 44" by 39"

$1,000-$1,500

Benches

Arts & Crafts bench
with a rectangular top over a horizontal stretcher with through-tenon details, original finish, 40" by 15" by 20"

$900-$1,100

Arts & Crafts bench
slab sides with recovered seat over a lower shelf with keyed tenon construction, worn original finish, 23" by 10" by 20"

$200-$300

Michigan Chair Co. hall bench
spindled sides over a solid seat, original finish, signed with paper label, crack to one slat, 24" by 17" by 31"

$600-$700

Roycroft bench
rectangular seat supported by heavy slab sides, partially stripped finish, unsigned but numbered A203, repair to one side. 47" by 17" by 25"

$1,400-$1,800

Arts & Crafts small bench

with three applied medallions to cutout sides. Overcoated original finish, some looseness. 17" by 19" by 13 1/2"

$300-$350

Limbert tall back Inglenook bench

with lift seat, the back and seat panels upholstered with original tacked-on Japan leather. Original finish with overcoat, wear and tears to seat leather. Branded mark. 47" by 48" by 20"

$1,200-$1,700

Michigan Chair Co.

The Michigan Chair Co. began as the Grand Ledge (Mich.) Chair Co. in 1883. The firm was in business for almost 100 years, closing in 1981.

Gustav Stickley piano bench

with cutout handles to plank sides, plank top and broad up-ended cross-stretcher. Good original finish and condition. Red decal. 22" by 36" by 12 3/4"

$3,800-$4,200

L. & J.G. Stickley hall bench
with hinged seat compartment, columnar vertical slats to back and arms, and long corbels under the apron. Original finish, minor edge wear. Handcraft decal. 37" by 42" by 18"

$5,500-$6,500

L. & J.G. Stickley piano bench
No. 211, with overhanging top, slatted sides and broad cross stretchers. Original finish, wear to top, good condition. "The Work of..." label. 22 1/2" by 40" by 15 1/2"

$1,500-$2,200

Bookcases

Arts & Crafts bookcase
double-door form with two vertical mullions at top, six adjustable shelves, original finish. 47" by 13" by 58"

$400-$500

Arts & Crafts bookcase
in the manner of Limbert, two-door form with six glass panes per door over open shelves on sides with cutout design at top, some wear to original finish, pegs added to top. 50" by 12" by 55"

$2,000-$2,400

Arts & Crafts revolving bookcase
slatted sides with adjustable shelf on one end, refinished, needs gluing. 18" by 19" by 34"

$175-$225

Lifetime bookcase
No. 7604, three-door form with six glass panes to each door and original copper hardware, slab sides with keyed tenon construction, original finish, signed, 60" by 12" by 45"

$4,000-$5,000

Limbert bookcase
similar to No. 315, in ash, double-door form with original iron hardware, slab sides with key and tenon construction, refinished, unsigned, restoration to back. 44" by 14" by 56"

$1,000-$1,400

Gustav Stickley bookcase
No. 717 1/2, open case having four fixed shelves with slab sides and through-tenon construction, lightly cleaned original finish, signed with red decal and paper label. 48" by 13" by 56"

$6,000-$7,000

Stickley Bros. bookcase
No. 4758, early two-door form with eight panes per door, original copper hardware, original dark finish, signed with paper label. 38" by 14" by 57"

$1,500-$2,000

Arts & Crafts single-door bench-made bookcase
with gallery top, yellow-painted interior and hammered copper lock plate. 57" by 24" by 16"

$700-$800

Arts & Crafts double-door bookcase

with gallery top, faux-mullion latticework to doors, and six interior shelves. Original finish, worn shelves are pine edged with oak, some duct tape on doors. Unmarked. 58 1/2" by 58" by 12 1/2"

$950-$1,250

Arts & Crafts two-door bookcase

possibly by Charles Stickley, with gallery top and chamfered back, eight glass panes to each door, and three interior shelves. Original finish, some looseness. Unmarked. 56" by 47" by 15"

$1,600-$1,800

Arts & Crafts double-door bookcase

in the style of Gustav Stickley, with gallery top, paneled back, eight-pane mullioned glass doors, and three stationary shelves. Original finish, seam separation, shrinkage to door. Carved urn mark, with "Ursinus" (for Ursinus College, Collegeville, Pa.). 58" by 50 1/4" by 12 3/4"

$1,800-$2,200

Banner revolving bookcase

(Canton, Ohio) each side with three compartments bordered by four slats. Original finish, seam separation to top. Stenciled mark. 47 1/2" by 23 3/4" square

$800-$1,000

Grand Rapids Mission four-section stacking bookcase
with faux-mullion latticework to glass-front panels. Original finish. Triangular G.R.M.
paper label. 54 1/2" by 34 3/4" by 12 1/2"

$650-$800

Grand Rapids two-door bookcase
with flush top, twelve panes per door, and three interior shelves. Excellent original finish,
missing three shelves. Marked with tag. 48" by 48" by 12"

$900-$1,100

Liberty triple bookcase
(English) with gallery top with spade-shaped cutouts, original leaded glass center door
with hammered copper pull, and three shelves on either end. Original finish, good
condition. Branded 2633, signed "Liberty" on the lock set. 47" by 71" by 10 1/4"

$5,500-$6,500

Lifetime two-door bookcase

circa 1910-15, oak, refinished, original glass and hardware, divided interior with two shelves on each side, overhanging top, made in Grand Rapids, Mich. 46" by 52" by 14"

$2,500-$3,000

Lifetime triple-door bookcase

with gallery top, glass panel doors, and hammered copper pulls, on casters. Original finish. Unmarked. 57" by 56 1/2" by 13"

$1,800-$2,200

Onondaga Shops three-door bookcase

with gallery top and 12-pane doors with hammered copper escutcheons. Refinished, good condition, split to one tenon. Unmarked. 56 1/2" by 74" by 11 3/4"

$7,000-$8,000

Roycroft single-door bookcase

with gallery top, chamfered back, and lower shelf fastened with keyed through-tenons. Very good restored original condition, some minor touch-ups, some paint splattering to back. Carved "Roycroft." 71 1/2" by 39 1/4" by 16"

$10,000-$12,000

Roycroft single-door bookcase
from the Roycroft Inn library with paneled back, original beveled glass pane, and blind bottom drawer. (Shelves not pictured.) Refinished, good condition and color. Carved orb and cross marks, and Roycroft. 60 1/2" by 31 1/4" by 15 1/2"

$12,000-$14,000

Gustav Stickley single-door bookcase
with gallery top and 16 glass panes, hammered iron V-pull. Good original finish and condition. Paper label and red decal. 56" by 35" by 13 1/4"

$6,000-$7,000

Gustav Stickley double-door bookcase
designed by Harvey Ellis, with paneled back, 12 square leaded glass panes to each door over three vertical panes, eight shelves and arched toe board. Excellent original finish and condition, minor scratches, hinge pins and escutcheons missing. Red decal. 58" by 59 1/2" by 14"

$17,000-$20,000

Gustav Stickley double-door bookcase
with gallery top, eight glass panes to each door with hammered copper V-pulls, and three interior shelves, the top and bottom mortised through the sides. Refinished, small chip to apron. Red decal and Craftsman paper label. 56 1/4" by 42 3/4" by 13"

$4,000-$5,000

Gustav Stickley two-door bookcase
1910, with gallery top, nine panes to each door, and hammered copper hardware. Cleaning to original finish, replaced toe boards, and glue blocks. Red decal and paper label. 56" by 60" by 13"

$6,500-$7,500

Gustav Stickley two-door bookcase
with gallery top mortised through the sides with keyed tenons, eight panes to each door and hammered copper V-pulls. Refinished. 56" by 51" by 13"

$5,500-$6,500

Gustav Stickley two-door bookcase
with gallery top, eight panes to each door and hammered copper V-pulls. Excellent original finish and condition. Paper label and red decal. 56" by 43" by 13"

$7,000-$8,000

Gustav Stickley two-door bookcase
with gallery top, eight panes to each door, and hammered iron V-pulls. Missing one pane of glass, restoration to finish, a few scratches and chips, back delaminating. Red decal. 56 1/2" by 48" by 13 1/2"

$3,500-$4,500

Gustav Stickley two-door bookcase
with gallery top, top and base mortised through the sides with keyed through-tenons, and two six-pane doors with hammered copper V-pulls. Original finish. Red decal. Paper label. 44" by 39" by 12"

$5,500-$7,000

Gustav Stickley two-door bookcase
with gallery top, three interior shelves, eight panes per door with hammered copper V-pulls, the top and bottom keyed-through the sides. Refinished, restoration to several small holes in front, loss to through-tenons at bottom and restoration to one at top. Recent paper label. 56" by 46" by 13"

$2,800-$3,250

Gustav Stickley two-door bookcase
with gallery top, eight glass panes per door, and three interior shelves, its top and base mortised through the sides. Refinished, filled-in holes to front divider and to doors around hardware. Faint red decal. 56 1/4" by 42 3/4" by 13 1/4"

$4,700-$5,200

Gustav Stickley two-door bookcase
with gallery top, eight glass panes to each door, the top and base keyed through the sides. Restored and enhanced original finish, warp to door. Unmarked. 56 1/4" by 51" by 13"

$4,500-$5,500

Gustav Stickley two-door bookcase
with gallery top and eight glass panes to each door, with V-pulls. (Unusual form with flush through-tenons). Overcoated finish. Outline of paper label. 56" by 48" by 13"
$5,000-$6,000

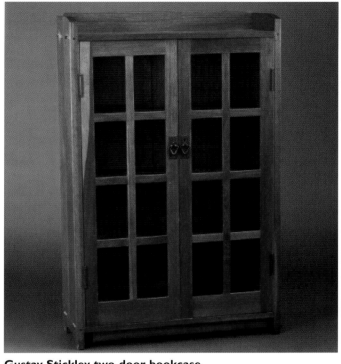

Gustav Stickley two-door bookcase
with gallery top, eight glass panes to each door (two replaced), hammered copper V-pulls and three interior shelves, with top and base mortised through the sides. (A rare size.) Light overcoated finish, shallow screw holes to doors (inside and out), burn to bottom left, crack to one rear leg. Branded Stickley. 56" by 34 3/4" by 12 3/4"
$3,000-$4,000

Gustav Stickley two-door mahogany bookcase
designed by Harvey Ellis, circa 1904-05, with overhanging top, pilaster posts, arched apron, and two long panes topped by two leaded square panes on each door, with key lock and three interior shelves. Refinished. Remnant of paper label. 58" by 42" by 14"
$7,500-$8,500

Gustav Stickley two-door mitered-mullion bookcase
with gallery top, eight panes to each door and hammered copper ring pulls. Good condition, skinned original finish (or heavily cleaned). Large red decal. 56" by 35 1/4" by 12 1/4"
$10,000-$12,000

L. & J.G. Stickley single-door bookcase
No. 641, with gallery top and keyed through-tenons. Refinished, good condition, two drill holes to back. Unsigned. 54 1/2" by 30" by 12"

$3,500-$4,500

L. & J.G. Stickley two-door bookcase
No. 637, with hammered copper pulls, overhanging top and arched apron. Original finish. good condition, crack to veneer on left side. "The Work of..." label. 55" by 36" by 13 3/4"

$2,700-$3,200

L. & J.G. Stickley two-door bookcase
with gallery top, 12 panes to each door with hammered copper pulls, the top and base mortises keyed through the sides. Good original finish. Handcraft decal. 55" by 52" by 12"

$5,500-$6,500

L. & J.G. Stickley three-door bookcase
with gallery top, keyed through-tenons, and 12 panes to each door. Original finish, missing locks, chip to rear left foot. Branded mark. 55" by 73" by 12"

$10,000-$12,000

Bookstands

Arts & Crafts bookstand
adjustable top shelf with ledge above a lower shelf slab sides with keyed-tenon construction, refinished. 32" by 13" by 30"

$225-$275

Arts & Crafts bookstand
V-trough above two lower shelves with slatted sides, refinished. 27" by 10" by 32"

$400-$450

Roycroft Little Journeys bookstand
with complete set of Little Journeys Memorial Edition books, original finish, signed with metal plate. 26" by 14" by 26"

$400-$500

Arts & Crafts rattan magazine holder
basket form with woven base and handle, natural finish. 22" by 15" by 18"

$90-$110

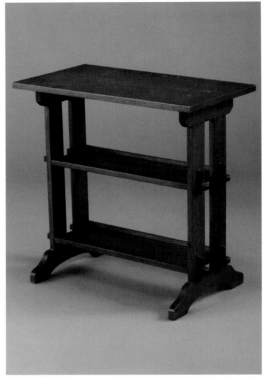

Michigan Chair Co. bookstand
with rectangular top, slatted sides, and three lower shelves. 34 1/2" by 18" by 14 1/4"

$250-$350

Roycroft Little Journeys bookstand
with keyed through-tenon shelves. Good original finish, some staining to top. Roycroft metal tag. 26 1/2" by 26" by 14"

$600-$800

Boxes

Arts & Crafts oak hinged box
with two handles and riveted strap hardware. Skinned finish. Unmarked. 8 1/4" by 15" by 12"

$300-$400

Gustav Stickley blanket box
with hinged and paneled top, panels to front and back, and spindled sides. Refinished. Eastwood paper label. 16" by 30" by 16"

$4,500-$5,000

Breakfront

Stickley Bros. breakfront
No. 8700, early form with two glass front cabinets flanking a single shelf and plate rail over a base cabinet consisting of a single door and two half drawers over a full drawer, original copper hardware, fine original finish, numbered. 60" by 24" by 56"

$3,800-$4,200

Buffet

Stickley Bros. buffet
No. 8610, English-influenced form with slatted gallery and plate rail above two half drawers and an open compartment over a full drawer, original brass strap hardware, original finish, minor stains, remnant of paper label. 54" by 21" by 46"

$3,500-$4,000

Cabinets

Arts & Crafts cabinet
leaded glass door with stylized floral design and an upper and lower drawer, keyed tenon construction at sides, restoration to top, handle replaced. 25" by 13" by 47"
$850-$1,000

Arts & Crafts cabinet
probably Austrian, two paneled doors with central panel in copper repousse, interior contains two shelves, original finish, minor veneer loss. 32" by 20" by 39"
$400-$500

Continental Secessionist mahogany cabinet
circa 1910, with exotic wood and mother-of-pearl inlay to case, double-doors with bevel-edged glass panes enclosing two interior shelves, cabinets and two open display areas, with brass hardware and details. Fine original condition. Unmarked. 77" by 59" by 18 1/2"
$3,500-$4,000

Charles Robert Ashbee

The British Guild and School of Handicraft was founded by architect Charles Robert Ashbee (1863-1942). Although Ashbee was a proponent of Gothic Revival architecture, he also promoted the work of Frank Lloyd Wright and the American Prairie School.

C.R. Ashbee pine music cabinet
for The Guild and School of Handicraft, circa 1899, its top and sides mortised with square tenons, elaborate brass hardware, Moorish cutout base, and interior shelves. Good new finish and condition. Unmarked. 49" by 19" by 14 1/2"
$12,000-$14,000

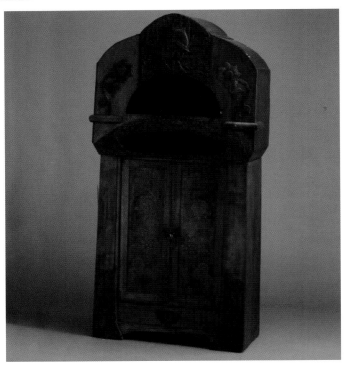

Scottish baronial-style two-piece cabinet

with repousse decoration of a knight and flowers, and a two-door cabinet with carved and polychromed strawberries and flowers, metal backplates, corner panels, and escutcheon. Original finish, some veneer chips and lifting, seam separations, tears to metal. Unmarked. 74" by 37" by 17"

$2,200-$2,500

Gustav Stickley piano roll cabinet

with two paneled doors and iron V-pulls. Original finish, some finish loss to front. Red decal inside left, paper label on back. 51" by 33" by 18"

$7,000-$8,000

Gustav Stickley cabinet

with gallery top, single panel door with iron V-pull, the interior fitted with three adjustable shelves. Original finish, missing back. Shadow of a decal inside left. 47" by 20" by 16 1/2"

$2,500-$3,500

Gustav Stickley spool cabinet

with eight drawers with wooden pulls. Cleaned original finish, repair to chip on drawer front. Red decal. 17 1/2" by 14" by 15"

$4,000-$4,800

Cellarettes

Arts & Crafts cellarette
tapered cabinet with fall front that opens to reveal revolving bottle rack, original finish. 20" by 16" by 38"

$300-$400

Gustav Stickley cellarette
with flush top, pull-out copper shelf, drawer and paneled cabinet door with copper pulls. Original finish, veneer lifting on sides and back. Large red decal. 39 1/2" by 22" by 16"

$3,500-$4,000

L. & J.G. Stickley cellarette
with single drawer, pull-out copper-lined shelf, and lower cabinet with interior fittings. Refinished, missing lock, crack to stretcher and door, old shellac repair to left side. Handcraft decal. 40" by 22" by 16"

$2,500-$3,000

L. & J.G. Stickley cellarette
with arched backsplash, pull-out copper shelf and two-door cabinet with hammered copper strap hinges and ring pulls. Original finish to base, top refinished. "The Work of..." decal. 35 1/2" by 32" by 16"

$10,000-$14,000

Chairs, Arm

Harden armchair
(Camden, N.Y.) five vertical slats at back and four under each arm, through-post construction, recovered original spring cushion, recoated original finish. 28" by 24" by 39"

$225-$300

Limbert armchair
No. 643, four vertical slats to back and single flared slat under each arm with spade cutouts, original drop-in seat and back cushions, original finish, branded, paper label. 30" by 39" by 37"

$1,500-$1,800

Limbert armchair
and rocker, Nos. 3663 and 3664, curved and flared back slats under an arched top rail, fluted legs with through-tenon construction, recovered original spring cushion, recoated original finish, branded signature, rocker 28" by 30" by 34", armchair 28" by 25" by 37"

$900-$1,200/pair

Prairie School armchair
in mahogany, large form with fluted legs with back supports, reupholstered back and seat, worn original finish. 30" by 28" by 38"

$250-$350

Shop of the Crafters armchair
(Cincinnati, Ohio, active 1904-20) peaked top with cutout over two flared cutout slats, worn original green leather upholstery, signed with paper label, original finish. 26" by 23" by 42"

$400-$500

Gustav Stickley armchair
No. 353A, in mahogany, Harvey Ellis influence, three vertical slats at back, over a worn original rush seat and arched seat rail, refinished, unsigned. 25" by 21" by 41"

$250-$350

L. & J.G. Stickley armchair
No. 408, Prairie School influence with eight curved slats at back and six under each arm, through-tenon construction, recovered original cushion, fine original finish, branded "The work of..." 25" by 25" by 32"

$6,000-$7,000

L. & J.G. Stickley armchair
similar to No. 816, open-arm form with six vertical slats at back, reupholstered leather cushion, refinished, signed "The Work of..." 27" by 23" by 39"

$300-$400

Arts & Crafts armchair
with vertical slats to back and sides, crest rail and top posts carved with quatrefoil, and flared paddle arms, its spring seat re-upholstered in light green velvet. Refinished. Stenciled 794. 37 1/2" by 33" by 23 1/4"

$900-$1,100

Harden armchair
(Camden, N.Y.) with vertical slats on the back and under wavy arms, drop-in oilcloth seat. Original finish, good condition, minor edge scuffs. Unmarked. 38" by 29" by 21 1/2"

$1,200-$1,500

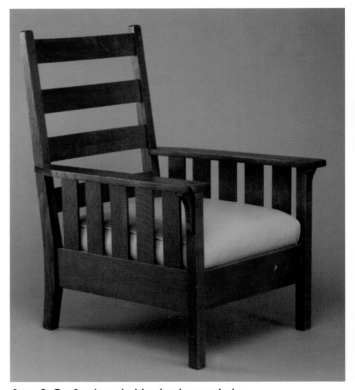

Arts & Crafts deep ladder-back armchair
with five slats to each side and new tan leather drop-in cushion. Original finish and condition, top of arms refinished. Unmarked. 41 1/2" by 29" by 30"

$900-$1,200

Harden wavy armchair

(Camden, N.Y.) with vertical slats to back and sides, and floral-upholstered fabric seat cushion. Original finish with overcoat, severe veneer chipping to leg bottoms. Paper tag. 38 1/2" by 29 1/2" by 24"

$700-$900

Harden oversized armchair

and rocker (Camden, N.Y.) with vertical slats under wavy arms, and drop-in spring seats. Refinished, good condition. Paper label on rocker. 41" by 30 1/2" by 28 1/2", and 40" by 30 1/2" by 35"

$2,500-$3,500/pair

Lifetime armchair

with three vertical slats to back and under the arms, long corbels, and original Japan leather upholstered seat cushion. Original finish to body, tops of arms refinished, minor tears to leather. 40 1/2" by 23 1/2" by 21"

$300-$400

Limbert armchair

with broad back slat and brown leather seat. Original finish. 36" by 26 1/2" by 18"

$150-$200

Limbert armchair

with angled back, corbels under flat paddle arms, scooped apron, and brown leather-upholstered seat and back cushions. (Back cushion not pictured). Original medium-brown finish, worn on arms. Branded mark. 32 1/2" by 31 1/2" by 34"

$2,500-$3,000

Limbert Ebon-Oak armchair

from the Mission Inn, inlaid with mission bell motif to back slat and geometric forms with post with brown leather drop-in seat. Original finish, good condition. 41" by 28" by 25 1/2"

$4,000-$5,000

Two Limbert chairs

one arm- and one side-, each with caned back and seat, and cutout trefoil on crest rail. Good original finish, replaced cane. Partial paper label. Armchair: 39 1/2" by 21 1/2" by 21", side chair: 39 1/2" by 18" by 12"

$1,000-$1,200/pair

Old Hickory barrel armchair

with woven split-cane seat and back. Original finish, minor splits to caning. Branded mark. 34 1/2" by 30 1/2" by 23"

$500-$600

Pair of armchairs
attributed to Phoenix (?), with vertical slats on back and under flat arms, and new brown leather drop-in seats. Original finish with light overcoat, good condition. 35" by 30" by 24 1/2"

$1,100-$1,500/pair

Pair of Roycroft armchairs
with broad crest rail, angular arms and tacked-on hard leather seat. Excellent new finish and good condition, new leather upholstery. Carved orb and cross mark. 38" by 23" by 22 1/4"

$3,000-$3,500/pair

Scottish baronial-style armchair
with copper repousse back plate with pheasant figure, copper arm lining and corner brackets, square cut-outs, reupholstered back panel, seat and armrests, on tapered legs. Refinished, veneer lifting and seam separations, some looseness. Unmarked. 41 1/2" by 25" by 24 1/4"

$1,200-$1,500

Gustav Stickley armchair
1902-04, with open sides and original tacked-on dark brown leather seat and back. Excellent original finish and condition, leather in great condition. Full box decal. 36 3/4" by 26" by 22 1/2"

$7,000-$8,000

Gustav Stickley armchair
Harvey Ellis design (arched skirts and tapering legs are common elements in Ellis designs), circa 1912-15, oak, worn original finish, red or black mark. 41" by 24 1/2" by 21"

$1,000-$1,200

Gustav Stickley armchair
with inverted-V crest rail, broad second slat, arched front and back stretchers, flaring legs and burgundy leather-upholstered seat. Original finish, some looseness. Unmarked. Very rare. 37 1/2" by 23 1/4" by 21 1/2"

$16,500-$18,000

Gustav Stickley child's armchair
with three horizontal back slats and original leather seat and tacks. Excellent original finish, normal wear to leather. Red decal and Craftsman mark. 26" by 18" by 14"
$1,500-$1,700

Gustav Stickley fixed-back armchair
No. 324, with slats to the seat rail and corbels under the arms, and new brown leather loose cushions. Original finish with overcoat. Red decal. 41" by 29" by 31"
$1,700-$2,000

Gustav Stickley ladder-back armchair
with scooped crest rail, "cloud-lift" apron, and woven cane seat. Excellent original dark finish, one minor split to caning. Red decal. 39" by 23" by 21"
$3,500-$4,500

'Cloud-lift'

The term "cloud-lift" refers to the modification of a traditional arched stretcher or apron by giving the bottom edges a straight— rather than curving— profile at the ends. This design motif can often be seen in early Chinese furniture forms.

Gustav Stickley ladder-back armchair
with five short vertical slats to each side, and red velvet-upholstered cushions (worn). Worn original finish, loose glue joints. Signed inside seat rail. 31" by 29" by 31"
$900-$1,200

Gustav Stickley ladder-back armchair
No. 310 1/2, with open arms and remnants of original tacked-on leather to seat rail. Worn original finish, scratches along one back leg, some looseness. Unmarked. 37 1/4" by 26 1/2" by 22"

$400-$600

Prairie School

The Prairie School of design derived from the publication in 1901 of "A Home in a Prairie Town," which architect Frank Lloyd Wright designed for the Ladies' Home Journal. Designs themes included horizontal forms and abstract geometric elements.

Gustav Stickley tall spindle-back armchair
with spindles to the floor and long corbels under the arms and tan leather loose cushion on sling seat. Excellent original finish, normal wear to front stretcher, one replaced spindle to back. Small red decal. 49" by 27" by 22"

$4,000-$5,000

Gustav Stickley "Thornden" armchair
with two horizontal back slats, narrow arms, and replaced seat. Original finish, minor wear to edges, replaced seat, a little loose. 1902-04. Red decal. 37" by 21" by 21 1/2"

$2,500-$3,000

Pair of Gustav Stickley V-back armchairs
with five vertical back slats, front legs mortised through the arms, and fabric-covered drop-in seat. Good condition, partially refinished with color added. Unmarked. Each 37 1/4" by 26 1/4" by 21"

$1,200-$1,500/pair

Pair of Gustav Stickley V-back armchairs
each with five vertical back slats and new maroon leather cushion. One overcoated, the other with added color and finish to arms. One bears red decal. Each 36" by 26" by 22"

$1,600-$1,900/pair

L. & J.G. Stickley armchair

No. 408, with vertical slats to floor, curved on back, and original brown leather drop-in seat cushion. Original finish, minor roughness to back, tear to cushion. "The Work of..." label. 32" by 26" by 27"

$4,200-$4,800

L. & J.G. Stickley bow-arm chair

No. 482, with arched apron and green suede upholstery. Original finish, good condition. "The Work of..." label under arm. 39" by 31" by 30"

$1,800-$2,400

L. & J.G. Stickley ladder-back armchair

with open arms and long corbels. Weathered finish, seam separation to leg, loose joints, no seat. Stenciled 818. 39" by 28" by 23"

$200-$300

Pair of L. & J.G. Stickley tall-back armchairs

each with four vertical back slats, open arms and green leather upholstered seat cushion. Restored original finish, good condition. 44" by 28" by 23"

$1,400-$1,800/pair

Set of six L. & J.G. Stickley/Onondaga Shops ladder-back armchairs

the seats re-upholstered in brown leather. Good original finish and condition, normal wear to arm tops, some nicks, chips and scratches (saw mark on one). Onondaga Shops paper label. 36 1/2" by 26" by 21"

$6,000-$7,000/set

Stickley Bros. fixed-back armchair

oak, original finish, drop-in seat, 41" tall, 27 1/2" wide

$600-$700

Chairs, Dining

Set of five Arts and Crafts dining chairs
four side- and one arm-, each with broad vertical back slat and red chenille-upholstered seats. Unmarked. Each 37" by 18" by 16"

$600-$800/set

Set of six English Arts & Crafts dining chairs
five side- and one arm, each with three vertical back slats and heart cutout and fabric seat cushion. Armchair (not pictured) has break to arm. Each (except arm) 41" by 17 1/2" by 16 1/2"

$900-$1,200/set

Set of six Liberty & Co. dining chairs
with tapering tongue-and-groove backs, paneled seats
and chamfered legs. (Includes set of cushions covered in
William Morris-designed fabric.) Each 43 1/2" by 17"
by 16 1/2"

$2,800-$3,300/set

Set of four Limbert dining chairs
of straight-cut oak, each with spade-shaped cut-outs, plank seat, and keyed-through stretcher. Refinished. Unmarked. Each 38"
by 17" by 18 1/2"

$3,000-$3,500/set

Set of six Stickley Bros. ladder-back dining chairs
two arm- and four side-, with replaced tacked-on brown vinyl seats. Good original finish, some looseness. Unmarked.
Armchair: 29" by 28" by 17 1/2"

$2,200-$3,000/set

Set of six Stickley Bros. dining chairs
two arm- and four side-, each with corseted crest rail, three vertical back slats, and tacked-on brown leather seat pad. Skinned medium finish. Quaint decal, stenciled number to several. Armchairs: 39" by 25" by 19", side chairs: 37 1/2" by 18 1/4" by 16"

$2,400-$3,000/set

Chairs, Hall

Jamestown Furniture unusual tall-back hall chair
(New York) in the style of Charles Rohlfs, with carved and cutout details, round rivets, and plank seat. Original finish to legs and back, seat is refinished. Unmarked. 56" by 16" by 13 3/4"

$500-$700

Limbert hall chair
with triangular cut-outs in sides and back, and plank seat. Refinished, good condition. Branded mark. 45" by 14" by 15"

$3,500-$4,500

Rohlfs high-back hall chair
with cutout horizontal back slat over a plank seat. Original finish, some paint stains and smudges, wood deterioration to shoe feet, missing some screw covers, seam separations to seat. Carved 1903 mark. 46" by 17" by 18"

$2,500-$3,000

Scottish baronial-style hall chair
in eagle design. Refinished, some looseness, lifting veneer. Unmarked. 42" by 19" by 17"

$800-$1,000

L. & J.G. Stickley hall chair
with vertical back slats, open arms and long corbels, with black leather-upholstered seat cushion. Overcoated original finish, minor looseness. Branded "The Work of..." 47" by 28" by 23"

$1,800-$2,200

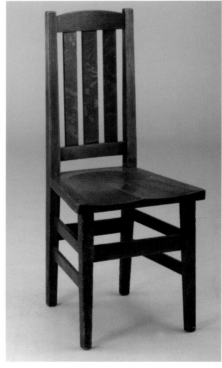

Stickley Bros. hall chair
with three vertical back slats and plank seat. Original finish, good condition, slightly loose. Unmarked. 38 1/4" by 16 1/4" by 15 1/4"

$250-$300

Chairs, Morris

Gustav Stickley Morris chair

No. 332, flat arm form with five slats under each arm, original facetted pegs, refinished, signed with red decal, replaced leather cushions. 31" by 36" by 39"

$4,200-$4,800

Gustav Stickley Morris chair

No. 367, 17 spindles under a straight arm, replaced seat foundation and cushion, refinished, unsigned. 30" by 36" by 37"

$3,500-$4,000

Arts and Crafts Morris chair

with horizontal back slats and original, worn laced leather cushions. Original finish, good condition, loose. 40" by 30" by 35"

$800-$900

Onondaga Shops Morris chair

No. 798, with slats to the floor and through-tenon construction, corbels and leather-upholstered cushions. Original finish with light overcoat, good condition. 41" by 31 1/2" by 36"

$4,000-$5,000

Gustav Stickley drop-arm Morris chair

with spindled sides and cushions re-upholstered in brown leather. Excellent original dark finish and condition, some wear to tops of arms. (Rare form.) Red decal. 40 1/2" by 33" by 37 1/2"

$30,000-$34,000

Gustav Stickley drop-arm Morris chair
with five vertical slats to each side, and cushions reupholstered in dark brown leather. Excellent original finish and condition, a couple of splits near tenons. Red decal. 38 1/2" by 32 3/4" by 37 1/2"

$12,000-$14,000

Gustav Stickley drop-arm Morris chair
No. 369, with five vertical slats and corbels under the arms, drop-in seat with new twill fabric upholstery. Refinished, good condition. Faint decal inside back leg. 38 1/2" by 33" by 38"

$6,500-$7,500

Gustav Stickley flat-arm Morris chair
1902-03, with scooped crest rail, slatted sides, and original tan leather scalloped-edged laced cushions. Excellent original finish and condition, perfect repair to hole in back of right arm. Stickley box decal. 39" by 31 1/2" by 36"

$17,500-$20,000

Gustav Stickley flat-arm Morris chair
No. 332, with slats to the floor, corbels under flat arms, and blue velvet upholstered cushion. Refinished, some replaced pegs, a few chips and restored veneer to leg bottoms. Unmarked. 40" by 31" by 38"

$3,500-$4,000

Gustav Stickley Morris chair
No. 332 with slats to the floor under flat arms, and original brown leather cushions.
Original finish, arms re-pegged and re-glued. Red decal. 39" by 31 1/2" by 36"
$5,000-$6,000

Gustav Stickley Morris chair
No. 2342, 1902-04, with vertical slats under flat arms, and (new) tan leather laced
cushions. Excellent original finish, minor roughness to bottom of legs. Decal, box mark.
46" by 36" by 31 1/2"
$12,000-$15,000

L. & J.G. Stickley bow-arm Morris chair
No. 416, with four short vertical slats to each side and long corbels, and drop-in spring
seat. Refinished, replaced pivot pegs, new leather. Co-joined label. 46" by 41" by 34"
$7,000-$8,000

L. & J.G. Stickley bow-arm Morris chair
with vertical slats under the arms and replaced green vinyl upholstery. Good original
finish and condition, some gouges to fronts of arms, and loose joints. "The Work of..."
label. 38" by 34" by 41 3/4"
$12,000 -$14,000

L.& J.G. Stickley Morris chair
with slats to the floor and long corbels under the arms, with original spring seat cushion reupholstered in ivory linen. Original finish, very minor crack to back support bar, some looseness. Unmarked. 38" by 34" by 37"

$4,250-$ 4,750

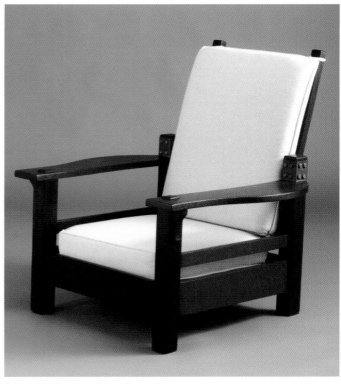

L.& J.G. Stickley Morris chair
with open paddle arms, strap leather back support with Stickley copper tacks, and new linen cushions. New dark finish, new leather strap. Unmarked. 38" by 37 1/2" by 33"

$1,500-$1,900

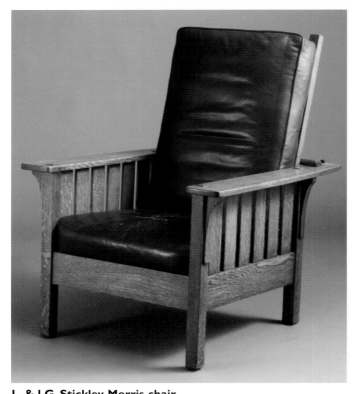

L. & J.G. Stickley Morris chair
with slats and short corbels under flat arms, and brown leather cushions. Original finish, good condition. "The Work of..." decal under arm. 40" by 32" by 35"

$2,500-$3,000

L. & J.G. Stickley open-arm Morris chair
with drop-in spring seat with replaced leather. Refinished, replaced reclining bar and pivot pegs. 41" by 32" by 36"

$1,500-$2,000

L. & J.G. Stickley paddle arm Morris chair
with long corbels and drop-in upholstered seat. Original finish, tops of arms overcoated, some looseness. Handcraft decal. 43" by 35" by 38"

$3,500-$4,000

L. & J.G. Stickley paddle-arm Morris chair
with long corbels and new tan suede cushions. Refinished. Handcraft decal on back stretcher. 37" by 35" by 38"

$4,000-$5,000

L. & J.G. Stickley/Onondaga Shops Morris chair
with square posts, open arms, short corbels and original brown leather cushions. Some wear to cushions, original finish, replaced front tenon caps on tops of arms. Unmarked. 40" by 32" by 36"

$2,000-$2,500

L. & J.G. Stickley/Onondaga Morris armchair
No. 790, with black leather support to back and Stickley copper tacks, riveted to square posts, flaring paddle arms, and beige linen seat and back cushions. Refinished, new cushions. Unmarked. 39" by 37" by 30"

$2,000-$2,500

Stickley Bros. child's Morris chair
with four horizontal back slats and drop in leather seat. Original finish, good condition.
Quaint tag. 34 1/2" by 21" by 23"

$650-$850

Stickley Bros. mahogany Morris chair
with single broad slat under each arm, arched apron, and new brown leather cushions.
Refinished. Metal Quaint tag. 42" by 30" by 35"

$1,800-$2,300

J.M. Young flat-arm Morris chair
(Camden, N.Y., 1890-1979) with four vertical slats to the floor and vinyl-upholstered
seat and back cushions. Original finish, good condition. Paper label. 37 1/2" by 30 1/2"
by 36 1/2"

$3,000-$3,750

J.M. Young Morris chair
(Camden, N.Y., 1890-1979) with slats to the floor and original laced brown leather
cushions. Original finish, excellent condition. Paper label. 42" by 31 1/2" by 36"

$3,000-$3,500

J.M. Young Morris chair
(Camden, N.Y., 1890-1979) circa 1910-15, oak, original finish, recovered leather cushion, with five slats to floor below arms (also found with three or four slats), unsigned. 33 1/2" by 38" by 40"

$3,800-$4,200

J.M. Young Morris chair
(Camden, N.Y., 1890-1979) circa 1910, with vertical slats under flat arms, mortised stretchers and (new) tan leather cushions. Refinished, excellent condition. Unmarked. 38 1/2" by 34 1/2" by 36 1/2"

$3,000-$3,500

Chairs, Other

Arts & Crafts tall-back chair
in mahogany, five vertical slats to back with arched seat rail and three slats under each arm, original finish, 26" by 25" by 46"

$150-$200

Arts & Crafts billiard chair
with three vertical slats to back, open arms and new brown leather seat cushion. Refinished, roughness to tops of arms, a little loose. 43" by 24 1/2" by 21 1/2"

$300-$400

Set of four Arts & Crafts billiard chairs
attributed to Heywood-Wakefield with flaring, pyramidal backposts and four vertical slats, saddle seats and footrests. Very good original finish, wear to footrests. Unmarked. 47" by 25" by 20"

$2,500-$3,000/set

Heywood Co.

The Heywood Co. (founded in 1826, Gardner, Mass.) merged with the Wakefield Rattan Co. in 1897. The firm manufactured and imported wicker furniture and accessories.

Plail Bros. barrel chair
(Wayland, N.Y., active 1906-1933) with spindles to the floor, and reupholstered seat cushion in vinyl. Original finish, break to back stretcher, chip to foot. Unmarked. 32 1/2" by 24 1/4" by 20"

$2,200-$2,600

Gustav Stickley slipper chair
Harvey Ellis design, circa 1904-06, mahogany, original finish, with seat rails, rope support missing, red mark. 36" tall, 18" wide, 18 1/2" deep

$500-$600

Set of four Stickley Bros. cafe chairs
each with heart-shaped cutout to horizontal back slat, and red leather-upholstered seat. Refinished. Stenciled 841 1/2, with Quaint decal. 28 3/4" by 16 1/2" by 15"

$1,000-$1,400/set

Chairs, Rockers

Limbert rocker
No. 642, four vertical slats with original drop-in seat and back cushions, original finish, branded, paper label. 22" by 32" by 33"

$225-$300

Limbert rocker
No. 644, four vertical slats to back and single flared slat under each arm with spade cutouts, original drop-in seat and back cushions, original finish, branded, paper label. 30" by 39" by 37"

$1,600-$2,000

Limbert rocker
No. 1646 3/4, with five slats to back under an arched top rail and five slats under each arm, recovered leather drop-in cushions, light recoat over original finish, minor repairs. 30" by 32" by 35"

$2,200-$2,700

Old Hickory rocker
woven seat and back on a twig frame, painted black, breaks to back and seat, signed Old Hickory, Martinsville, IN, 24" by 33" by 35"

$125-$175

Shop of the Crafters rocker
(Cincinnati, Ohio, active 1904-20) peaked top with cutout over two flared cutout slats, recovered cushion over a notched seat rail, original finish, unsigned. 26" by 32" by 39"

$400-$500

Gustav Stickley rocker
No. 2625, early form with five vertical slats over a roped foundation, replaced loose cushion, fine original finish, signed with red box mark, 27" by 28" by 38"

$700-$900

L. & J.G. Stickley rocker
No. 409, with six slats under each arm and eight curved slats at back, nicely recovered leather drop-in cushions, through-tenon construction, lightly recoated original finish, signed with Handcraft decal. 27" by 33" by 32"

$2,500-$3,000

Arts & Crafts rocker
original spring cushion, leather added over a slatted back, worn original finish. 26" by 30" by 34"

$200-$250

Arts & Crafts rocker
three horizontal slats to back, through-post construction on arms with corbel supports, recovered seat, original finish. 27" by 29" by 33"

$75-$125

Arts & Crafts child's rocker
three vertical slats with cutout design over a solid seat, original finish. 17" by 24" by 24"

$40-$60

Arts & Crafts child's rocker
six narrow vertical slats at back over a saddle seat, original finish, 17" by 28" by 29"

$300-$400

Harden wavy-arm rocker
(Camden, N.Y.) with slats to back and sides. Skinned finish, missing seat cushion, break to back leg. Harden paper tag. 36" by 29 3/4" by 31 1/4"

$750-$850

Harden rocker
(Camden, N.Y.) and armchair with vertical slats to back and under wavy arms, drop-in spring seats. Original finish, wear to arms on armchair. Paper labels on back stretchers. 36 1/2" by 29 1/2" by 31 1/2", and 38 1/2" by 29 1/2" by 24 1/4"

$2,500-$3,200/pair

Limbert open-arm Morris rocker
with corbels under long flat arms, arched aprons, and new beige linen cushions (back one not shown). Original finish. Branded mark. 32" by 31" by 40"

$2,750-$3,250

Limbert rocker
No. 317, with five vertical slats to back and sides, long corbels, arched aprons, and red vinyl-upholstered seat cushion. Good original finish. Branded mark. 35 1/2" by 30" by 31"

$1,600-$2,000

Onondaga Shops open-arm rocker
with six vertical slats under a crest rail, and drop-in seat. Original finish, minor wear.

$400-$600

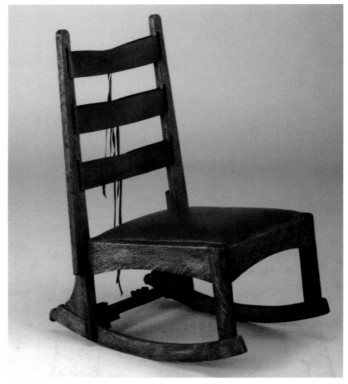

Rohlfs sewing rocker
with three horizontal hard leather bands to the back, arched apron, and corbels from back posts to rockers. Refinished. 35 1/2" by 17" by 27"

$600-$800

Roycroft chestnut sewing rocker
with five vertical back slats and tacked-on hard leather seat. Good condition, refinished, new leather. Carved orb and cross mark. 34" by 19 1/2" by 18"

$800-$900

Gustav Stickley humpback rocker
1902, oak, original finish, small mark, seat cover replaced, 38" tall, 28" wide

$1,600-$1,800

Gustav Stickley maple rocker
with three vertical back slats, original rush seat over arched apron. Original finish. Branded on outside back stretcher. 35 1/2" by 24" by 28 1/4"

$800-$900

Gustav Stickley open-arm rocker
with three vertical back slats and brown leather seat. Original finish, leather and tacks. Small red decal. 38" by 25 3/4" by 29 1/2"

$750-$1,000

Gustav Stickley rocker

with tall back, vertical slats under each arm, and fabric upholstered cushions. Skinned original finish, original springs, good condition. Branded mark. 41" by 29" by 33"

$2,500-$3,000

Gustav Stickley rocker

No. 317, circa 1912-16, oak, refinished, original seat frame and springs, new upholstery, black mark. 37 1/2" tall, 27" wide

$1,000-$1,250

Gustav Stickley rocker

with three vertical back slats, new paper-rush seat over arched apron. Stripped finish. Red decal. 35" by 24 1/2" by 28"

$400-$500

Gustav Stickley sewing rocker

with inverted-V crest rail topping ladderback, and non-original period brown leather cushion. Original finish with overcoat, some looseness, tears to leather. Unmarked. 33 1/2" by 18" by 22"

$300-$400

Gustav Stickley "Thornden"
sewing rocker with two horizontal planks to back and replaced rush seat. Original finish, a little loose. Small boxed red decal. 30 1/2" by 18" by 16"

$300-$400

Gustav Stickley V-back rocker
with five vertical back slats and rush seat. Original finish, new rush. Unmarked. 33 1/2" by 25 3/4" by 28"

$700-$800

Gustav Stickley V-back rocker
with five vertical back slats, open arms, and green vinyl covered seat. Worn original finish, replaced leather seat, loose joints. Unmarked. 35" by 26" by 24"

$550-$650

L. & J.G. Stickley high-back rocker
with six vertical slats to back and sides, and twill upholstered drop-in seat. Good original finish and condition. "The Work of..." branded mark. 38" by 28 1/2" by 32"

$3,000-$3,500

L. & J.G. Stickley open-arm rocker
with six vertical back slats and new dark brown leather-upholstered seat cushion. Worn original finish, good condition. "The Work of..." decal. 38" by 27 3/4" by 31 1/2"

$1,200-$1,500

L. & J.G. Stickley rocker
with vertical slats to back and sides, and yellow fabric-upholstered seat cushion. Original finish, recent oil application. "The Work of..." decal. 37 1/2" by 28 1/4" by 28 1/2"

$1,500-$2,000

L. & J.G. Stickley rocker
with vertical slats to back and arms, through-tenon construction, long corbels and upholstered drop-in cushion. Overcoated original finish, good condition. "The Work of..." decal. 38" by 28 1/2" by 31 1/2"

$1,500-$1,800

L. & J.G. Stickley rocker
with six vertical back slats, arms with through tenon construction and arched apron. (New drop-in seat, newly recovered in leather, not pictured.) Overcoated original finish, missing seat, some looseness. "The Work of..." decal. 35" by 28" by 29"

$550-$650

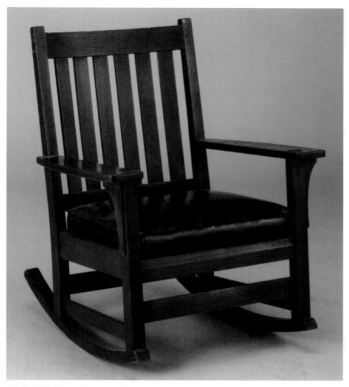

L. & J.G. Stickley rocker
with vertical back slats and drop-in seat with replaced leather. Original finish, good condition. Handcraft decal. 35" by 27" by 30"

$900-$1,100

L. & J.G. Stickley rocker
with six vertical slats to back, corbels under open arms, and original vinyl cushions (back cushion not pictured). Original finish with overcoat. "The Work of..." decal. 38" by 28" by 29"

$1,500-$1,900

L. & J.G. Stickley rocker
with slats and corbels under flat arms, and dark brown leather cushions. Refinished, some looseness at back arm joint. "The Work of..." label. 37" by 31" by 35"

$1,900-$2,400

L. & J.G. Stickley rocker
with six vertical back slats, open arms, and fabric covered seat. Original finish, good condition. "The Work of..." decal. 35" by 27" by 29"

$800-$1,000

L. & J.G. Stickley rocker
No. 409, with vertical slats to the floor, curved on back, and original brown leather seat cushions. Original finish, good condition. "The Work of..." label. 32" by 26" by 30"
$4,500-$5,000

Stickley Bros. mahogany rocker
with inlaid broad back panel, arched crest rails and apron, and brown leather seat cushion. Original finish to body, arms refinished, one piece of inlay replaced. Remnant of paper label. 42" by 26" by 30"
$1,400-$1,800

Stickley Bros. rocker
and armchair set, each with vertical back slats and newly upholstered drop-in seats. Original finish with overcoat. Quaint tag and paper label on armchair, partial paper label on rocker. 40" by 25 1/2" by 29", and 42" by 25 1/2" by 22"
$900-$1,100/pair

Stickley Bros. Quaint oversized rocker
(No. 604?), circa 1912-15, oak, original finish, metal tag. 36" tall, 33" wide, 33 1/2" deep
$1,800-$2,200

Chairs, Side

Limbert side chair
No. 641 1/2, four slats to back with original drop-in and
back cushion, original finish, branded, paper label. 22"
by 20" by 36"

$400-$500

Gustav Stickley side chair
No. 349 1/2, heavy ladder back form with three
horizontal slats at back over replaced leather seat,
refinished, signed with paper label. 18" by 18" by 38"

$250-$300

Gustav Stickley side chair
No. 353, Harvey Ellis influence, in mahogany, three
vertical slats to back above an arched seat rail and
replaced rush seat, original finish, signed with red decal.
17" by 17" by 40"

$150-$200

Two English Arts & Crafts side chairs
in walnut, inlaid circular design in wood and mother-of-
pearl, over a tooled leather back and seat, original finish,
leather seats damaged. Each 17" by 15" by 35"

$400-$500/pair

Pair of Old Hickory side chairs
with spindled backs and split reed seats. Excellent condition. Branded mark. Each 35 1/2" by 19 1/2" by 23"

$500-$600/pair

Onondaga Shops side chair
No. 788, with five vertical back slats under crest rail,
and new tacked-on leather seat. Original finish, good
condition. 35" by 17 1/2" by 16 1/2"

$350-$450

Charles Rohlfs ladder-back side chair
1906, back slats and apron rails all cut out with triangles,
drop-in seat upholstered in new leather. New dark finish,
repaired crack to rear right leg at seat. Red mark/date. 35
1/4" by 16" by 20"

$1,500-$1,800

Roycroft side chair
with four vertical back slats, Mackmurdo feet and
replaced leather upholstered seat. Original finish, good
condition. Orb and cross mark. 38" by 18" by 17"

$1,000-$1,500

Gustav Stickley curly maple side chair
designed by Harvey Ellis, with copper and pewter
inlay to back slats, inset rush seat, arched seat rails. Old
refinish, original rush, copper stem inlay missing from
one, a few veneer chips to stretchers. Unmarked. 40" by
17" by 17 1/2"

$3,200-$3,750

Gustav Stickley ladder-back side chair
No. 306 1/2, mahogany, refinished with replaced seat
and tacks, unmarked. 36" tall, 17" wide

$600-$700

Gustav Stickley high-back side chair
No. 350, oak, 1912, original finish, seat and tacks, black
mark. 39" tall, 17 1/2" wide

$650-$750

Gustav Stickley side chair
Harvey Ellis design (arched skirts and tapering legs are
common elements in Ellis designs), circa 1912-15, oak,
original finish. 39 1/2" by 17" by 17"

$800-$900

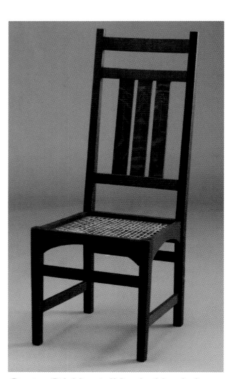

Gustav Stickley tall-back side chair
designed by Harvey Ellis, with three vertical back slats
inlaid with pewter and copper stylized flowers. New
finish, good condition, recaned seat foundation. No
visible mark. 43" by 17" by 21"

$6,000-$8,000

Gustav Stickley V-back side chair
with five vertical back slats and original tacked-on
leather seat. Cleaned original finish, crude restoration to
leather. Large paper label. 35 1/2" by 18 3/4" by 19"

$900-$1,200

Set of four Gustav Stickley ladder-back side chairs
with broad stretcher to front and back and double stretchers on the sides, the seats recovered in green vinyl. Refinished. Unmarked. 36" by 18" by 17"
$1,400-$1,600/set

Set of five Gustav Stickley side chairs
each with three horizontal back slats and tacked-on leather upholstered seats. Partially refinished. Red decal inside back stretchers. 36" by 17" by 16 1/2"
$2,500-$2,800/set

Set of five Gustav Stickley side chairs
and one armchair with three vertical back slats. Missing seats, original finish, good condition. Branded mark. 39 1/2" by 24 3/4" by 21"
$2,300-$2,800/set

Set of six Gustav Stickley side chairs
each with four vertical back slats and new leather cushions. Original finish, good condition, some looseness (normal wear from use). Branded mark. Each 39" by 18 1/2" by 17"

$4,000-$5,000/set

Set of six Gustav Stickley ladder-back side chairs
No. 306 1/2, each with original tacked-on brown leather seat. Cleaned original finish with worn and torn leather, chairs need regluing. Red decal. Each 36" by 17" by 16 1/2"

$2,000-$2,500/set

Pair of L. & J.G. Stickley spindle-back side chairs
No. 330, with original brown leather-covered seats. Original finish, minor chips. Handcraft decals. 36 1/2" by 16" by 15"

$1,600-$1,800/pair

Four L. & J.G. Stickley side chairs
with three vertical back slats and plank seats. Refinished, good condition. "The Work of..." decal remnants on three. Each 36" by 17 3/4" by 16 1/2"

$1,400-$1,800/set

L. & J.G. Stickley side chair
with three vertical back slats, missing seat. 35" by 17 3/4" by 16 1/2"

$150-$200

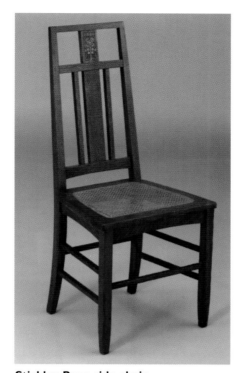

Stickley Bros. side chair
with three vertical back slats, center inlaid with Glasgow rose, and cane seat. Overcoated original finish, missing screw covers on back, some edge roughness. 40" by 17 1/2" by 15"

$700-$800

Stickley Bros. Quaint ladder-back side chair
circa 1910-15, oak, original finish, replaced leather seat and tacks, metal tag. 37 1/2" by 18 1/2" by 17"

$550-$650

Three Stickley Bros. side chairs
and one armchair with cutout back slats and stretchers, tacked-on original oilcloth. Original finish, tear to armchair upholstery, screw holes to some legs, loose. Armchair: 42" by 25 1/2" by 21 1/2"

$1,000-$1,300/set

Set of six Stickley Bros. side chairs
each with three vertical back slats, black leather-upholstered seat, and corseted front stretcher. Original finish with overcoat. Stenciled 479 1/2. Each 37" by 18 1/4" by 16"

$2,500-$3,200/set

Chaise

Arts & Crafts child's chaise
with slanted backrest and applied tenon details, worn original dark finish, some looseness. 41" by 19" by 18"

$80-$120

Chests

English pine tall chest
manufactured by T. Barker and Sons, 16 drawers with iron pulls and brackets, flush-tenon construction, refinished, signed with metal tag. 25" by 27" by 74"

$2,500-$3,000

Arts & Crafts blanket chest
with panel top and sides, with multiple butterfly joints on all panels, strap iron hardware and handles. Original finish with color added to top, good condition. 18" by 42" by 23"

$3,000-$4,000

Batchelder small chest
with incised daffodil front panel. Very good condition, small filled holes on top and front center, some color added. 13 3/4" by 27 1/2" by 14 1/2"

$6,700-$8,000

Ernest Batchelder

Ernest Batchelder was a native of New Hampshire, who studied at the Harvard Summer School of Design. Upon moving to California, Batchelder joined the department of Arts & Crafts at the Throop Polytechnic Institute in Pasadena in 1902. Eventually opening his own school in Pasadena in 1909, Batchelder enjoyed considerable success designing interiors, furniture and ceramics, especially hand-molded tiles, until the Depression ended his business. Batchelder died in Pasadena in 1957.

Greene & Greene oak and yellow pine double blanket chest
from the Pratt Residence, Ojai, Calif., its unusually mortised corners fastened with square dowel pegs, topped by two lift-top doors. Good original finish and condition. 18 1/2", 65" by 23 3/4"

$20,000-$25,000

The Greenes

Charles Sumner Greene (1868-1957) and Henry Mather Greene (1870-1954) gained fame as architects specializing in California bungalows. During their most prolific period, from 1902 to 1910, they also offered design services that included furniture and lighting.

Roycroft bridal chest
with broad wrought-iron hinges clasp and handles. Quarter sawn oak grain-painted to resemble rosewood. Fine original finish, possibly original lock. Carved orb and cross mark. 19" by 46" by 21 1/2"

$15,000-$17,000

Gustav Stickley early chest
with paneled back, two-over-four drawer configuation, and oval copper drop pulls. Stripped finish, some edge chips, one pull polished. Unmarked. 49 1/2" by 40 3/4" by 22 1/4"

$5,200-$5,800

Gustav Stickley four-drawer chest
designed by Harvey Ellis with attached pivoting mirror, round wooden pulls and arched apron. Refinished, veneer chips to right side. Red decal. 65" by 48" by 22"

$3,200-$3,800

Gustav Stickley five-drawer chest
No. 621, with iron pulls and paneled sides. Original finish, two back boards replaced. Black ink mark. 42" by 36" by 20 1/2"

$5,500-$6,500

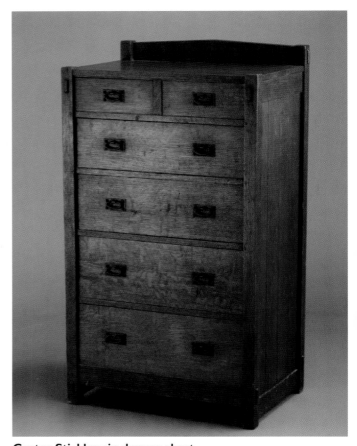

Gustav Stickley early five-drawer chest

with arched backsplash, paneled sides and back, and pyramidal wooden pulls. Original finish, seam separation to top, minor wear to legs, crack to one. Large red decal. 43" by 36" by 20"

$7,500-$8,500

Gustav Stickley six-drawer chest

with arched backsplash, paneled sides, and iron oval pulls. Cleaned original finish, some roughness to edges, small dents, scratches and stains to top. Remnant of decal and paper label. (Rare size.) 53" by 29" by 20"

$5,500-$6,500

Gustav Stickley six-drawer chest

with V backsplash, and oval copper pulls. Excellent original finish and color, slight bow and seam separation to top, sliver from right front post. Branded outside left drawer. 52 1/2" by 40" by 22"

$8,000-$9,000

Gustav Stickley nine-drawer chest

designed by Harvey Ellis with gallery top, tapered trapezoidal legs, mushroom pulls and arched apron. Original finish, good condition, small slice out of top edge, two small chips. Red decal inside top right drawer. 50 1/2" by 36" by 20"

$6,500-$7,500

Gustav Stickley nine-drawer chest

with backsplash, six small drawers over three graduated ones, all with hammered copper V-pulls, arched apron and sides. Stripped finish, veneer lifting and chipping and two drill holes on right side. Red decal inside drawer and paper label. 50" by 36" by 20"

$3,500-$4,000

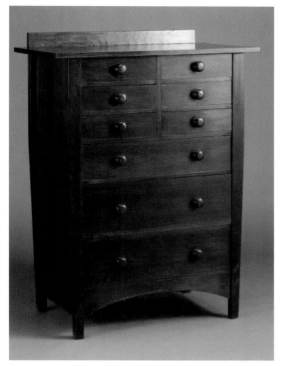

Gustav Stickley nine-drawer tall chest
designed by Harvey Ellis with backsplash, arched apron and sides, and
circular wooden pulls. Top and sides refinished, some flaking, veneer
repairs to both sides. Craftsman paper label. 50" by 36" by 20"
$3,000-$3,500

L. & J.G. Stickley four-drawer chest
No. 99, with arched backsplash and apron, paneled sides, and round wooden pulls. Original finish.
Handcraft label. 37" by 48" by 22"
$3,000-$4,000

L. & J.G. Stickley six-drawer chest
with arched backsplash and apron, paneled sides, and round wooden pulls. Original
finish. Minor chips. "The Work of..." label. 50" by 42" by 17 1/2"
$3,000-$3,500

China Cabinets

Arts & Crafts china cabinet
Prairie School influence, two-door form with plate rail at top, three shelves, original
finish. 42" by 15" by 62"
$500-$600

Onondaga Shops china cabinet
No. 605, in chestnut, single door with 12 panes of glass above a drawer with original
wood facetted knobs, chamfered back and shoe-foot base, original finish, unsigned. 44"
by 16" by 66"
$4,500-$5,200

Gustav Stickley china cabinet
No. 803, Harvey Ellis influence, single arched door over an arched toe board, V-board
back, refinished. 36" by 15" by 60"
$3,500-$4,000

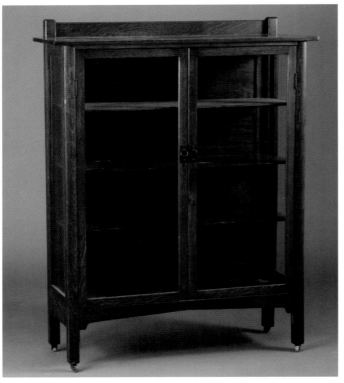

Arts & Crafts two-door china cabinet
with overhanging top, single glass pane to doors and sides, and three interior shelves. Original finish, replaced hardware. Stenciled 36. On casters: 58" by 44" by 15 1/4"

$1,200-$1,500

Arts & Crafts two-door china cabinet
with eight panes per door, four to sides, and three interior shelves. Original finish, good condition. Stenciled 141. 48 1/4" by 35 3/4" by 13"

$2,200-$2,600

Arts & Crafts china cabinet
with overhanging top, glass panel doors, with partial mirror-back and three interior shelves. Original finish, good condition. 58" by 49" by 16/ 1/2"

$700-$800

Arts & Crafts "side-by-side" china cabinet
with single glass door with faux-mullion latticework and three interior shelves, flanked by a drop-front desk over three drawers. Original finish, repair to back leg, back partly off, a few nicks. Unmarked. 57 1/2" by 39 3/4" by 12 1/2"

$550-$650

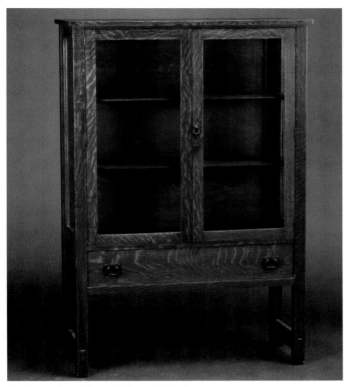

Lifetime two-door china cabinet
with single glass pane to doors and sides, two interior shelves and lower drawer, with hammered copper hardware. Good original finish. Decal. 58" by 39" by 15"
$3,000-$3,500

Limbert single-door china cabinet
with arched backsplash, three glass panes to door over one large, and open shelf on either side supported by long corbels, with three interior shelves. Good original finish. Faint stenciled number. On casters: 59" by 44 1/2" by 16 1/2"
$5,000-$6,000

Limbert two-door china cabinet
with two-over-three glass panes to each door and single pane to sides, arched apron and sides, with three interior shelves. Original finish, good condition. Branded mark and stenciled 1308. 55 3/4" by 30 1/2" by 14 1/4"
$3,000-$3,500

Paine Furniture Co. china cabinet
(Boston) with 12-pane glass doors over cabinet doors with brass strap hinges and brass hardware. Refinished, very good condition. Metal tag. 70" by 49 1/2" by 17"
$4,000-$4,800

Shop of the Crafters five-door china cupboard/bookcase
(Cincinnati, Ohio, active 1904-20) with beveled top, two small cabinets to each side, and applied faux mullion over the center glass panel. Restored original finish. 64" by 43" 15 1/2"

$2,300-$2,800

Gustav Stickley single-door china cabinet
with overhanging top and hammered copper V-pull. Original finish, some color loss to top, good condition. Red decal inside, remnants of paper label. 63" by 36" by 15"

$6,000-$7,000

Gustav Stickley single-door china cabinet
No. 820, with hammered copper pull on 12-pane door, overhanging top. Original key. Worn original finish. Red decal and paper label. 62 1/2" by 36" by 16 1/4"

$5,000-$6,000

Gustav Stickley single-door china cabinet
with 16 glass panes to door, and four to each side, with three fixed interior shelves and top and base mortised through the sides. Overcoated original finish, one screw hole, one broken pane of glass. Craftsman paper label. 57 3/4" by 35 1/4" by 13"

$5,200-$5,800

Gustav Stickley two-door china cabinet
with gallery top, eight panes to each door, and hammered copper V-pulls. Excellent original finish and condition. Paper label, red decal. 84 1/4" by 29 1/2" by 15"

$10,000-$14,000

Gustav Stickley two-door china cabinet
with backsplash and overhanging top, eight panes per door with hammered copper V-pulls, paneled interior with three shelves. Great original finish, four 1/4" drill holes on right to accommodate lighting. Branded mark and paper label. 63" by 42" by 15"

$5,500-$7,000

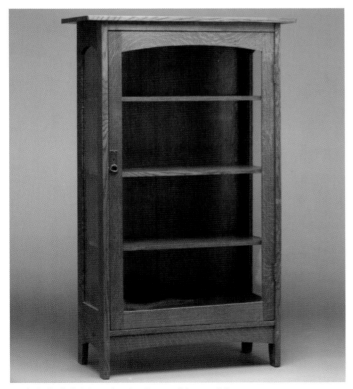

L. & J.G. Stickley single-door china cabinet
with overhanging top, arched doorframe and side panels, and three interior shelves. Fine original finish and condition. Handcraft mark. 60" by 36" by 16"

$5,500-$6,500

L. & J.G. Stickley single-door china cabinet
with paneled back, nine glass panes to door and three to each side, arched toe board and two interior shelves. Excellent original finish. "The Work of..." decal. 55" by 34" by 15"

$4,500-$5,000

L. & J.G. Stickley two-door china cabinet
with paneled back, six glass panes to each door and three to each side, with arched toe board. Excellent original finish. Numbered 285/728 in black. 54" by 47 1/2" by 15"
$5,500-$6,500

L. & J.G. Stickley two-door china cabinet
with overhanging rectangular top, leaded glass panes over single pane to doors and sides, with three interior shelves. Good original finish. Handcraft decal. 66" by 44" by 16"
$7,500-$8,500

L. & J.G. Stickley two-door china cabinet
with overhanging top, mullioned panes over a long glass panel on doors and sides, with one fixed interior plate shelf and two adjustable shelves. Refinished. Unmarked. 62" by 46" by 16"
$4,200-$5,000

Stickley Bros. china cabinet
with backsplash, interior mirror panel, and two glass pane doors with hammered brass hardware. Good original finish, water discoloration to two feet, minor nicks to edges. Branded Stickley Brothers, stenciled 8852. 59" by 46 1/2" by 15"
$1,500-$1,800

Clocks, Tall Case

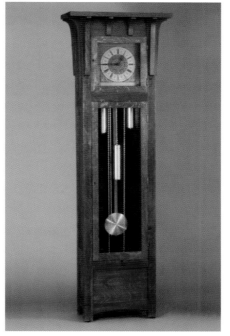

Tall case clock
attributed to Colonial Clock Co. (Holland, Mich.), with overhanging top on multiple corbels, circular etched copper face and glass panel door over pendulum door, weights and cylindrical chimes (several chimes no longer attached). Original finish. Unmarked. 84 1/2" by 27" by 15"

$1,850-$2,300

Shop of the Crafters tall case clock
(Cincinnati, Ohio, active 1904-20) with pendulum movement, chime and brass numerals, and slag glass paneled door concealing music drawers, topped by a pyramidal shade with slag glass panels. Original ebonized finish, crack to one glass pane on shade. Unmarked. 76" by 23" by 20"

$1,600-$1,800

Coat Rack

Costumers

Limbert costumer
No. 231, single pole with original copper hooks supported by a corbel cruciform base, original finish, branded, 16" by 16" by 71"

$450-$550

Charles Rohlfs tall case clock
with carved and cutout posts keyed through side panels, recessed circular dial with copper-painted numeral markers, copper hands and reticulated back plate, and rectangular cutouts to front door enclosing brass pendulum and cylindrical weight. Excellent original finish, minor delamination to bezel on left side of face, crack to front key, minor paint loss on hour markers, some delamination and veneer loss to back panel, new key for winding. Red-stained signature. 85 1/2" by 24" by 12"

$50,000-$60,000

Arts & Crafts coat rack
with four brass hooks. 69 1/2" tall

$200-$300

Arts & Crafts costumer
with shoe feet and cast double hooks. 67 1/2" tall

$400-$500

Gustav Stickley double costumer
1906, oak, refinished, missing one set of hooks, 72 1/2"
tall, 13" deep

$2,400-$2,600

Gustav Stickley double costumer
with tapering posts and six bronze double hooks.
Original finish, short seam separation and minor
checking, stain on one side. Unmarked. 71" by 12 1/2"
by 22"

$3,000-$4,000

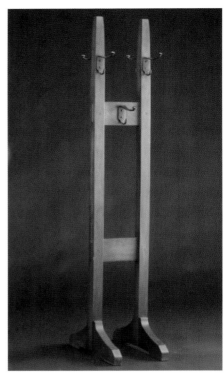

Gustav Stickley double costumer
1907-12, with tapering posts with six bronze double
hooks. Light cleaning to original finish, three hooks
replaced. Red decal. 73" by 13" by 22"

$2,000-$2,500

Gustav Stickley double costumer
Good original finish, one hook missing, seam separation
and looseness. Early red decal. 67 1/2" by 13 1/2"

$1,400-$1,800

Gustav Stickley costumer
with tapering post, four double wrought iron hooks and
pyramidal screws. Cleaned original finish. Red decal on
base. 71" by 22" square

$1,000-$1,500

Stickley Bros. double costumer
with two stretchers mortised through rounded posts,
with eleven hooks. Original finish, with scratches. Metal
tag. 68 1/2" by 17" by 22"

$850-$950

Desks

Arts & Crafts desk

in mahogany, spindle gallery over a drop front with strap hinges above a single drawer, complete interior, refinished. 34" by 16" by 53"

$800-$1,000

Arts & Crafts desk

rectangular top over a single drawer with original copper hardware and slatted book shelves at sides, refinished. 42" by 28" by 29"

$225-$275

Gustav Stickley desk

No. 710, rectangular top above central drawer and kneehole compartment, flanked by two half drawers with original copper hardware, paneled sides with flush-tenon construction, original finish, signed with red decal. 42" by 24" by 29"

$900-$1,100

Gustav Stickley desk

No. 720, in mahogany, two drawers with original brass hardware and letter organizer at back, stripped finish, unsigned, locks added. 38" by 23" by 37"

$1,000-$1,200

Gustav Stickley writing desk

No. 708, rectangular top above two drawers with original brass hardware, gallery missing and lower shelf cut back, refinished, remnant of decal, 40" by 22" by 30"

$300 to $350

Arts & Crafts desk

with square posts through the top and three drawers with square wooden pulls. Heavy overcoat to base, top refinished, one replaced knob. Stenciled number 486. 29 1/2", 48" by 28"

$125-$175

Arts & Crafts double-pedestal desk

with single drawer and bookcase shelf to each side with cutout grill, front and back. Original finish, veneer lifting and loss to top, some looseness. 30" by 42" by 46"

$200-$300

Arts & Crafts drop-front desk

with gallery top and interior gallery, with top and base mortised through the sides with keyed through-tenons, four drawers with wooden pulls, and open cabinet below. Original dark finish, seam separation and holes on right side. 48" by 38" by 15"

$2,800-$3,250

Arts & Crafts mahogany drop-front corner desk

with spindled open section, triangular pivoting drawer, and two-door cabinet with riveted strap brass hardware. Original finish and condition. Unmarked. 57" by 31" by 17"

$1,500-$1,700

Arts & Crafts telephone desk

and chair, circa 1912-15, oak, unmarked but probably made in Grand Rapids, Mich., original finish and cane seat. Desk: 34 1/2" tall, 22" wide, 15" deep

$550-$650/pair

Byrdcliffe mahogany knee-hole desk

with single drawer to one side and three drawers to the other, the side and back panels carved with mottos in Latin, Greek, and Italian (Ralph Radcliffe Whitehead's own desk). Accompanied by the original two-sided drawing for the Latin and Greek inscriptions. Excellent original finish all around, one replaced pull. 28 1/2" by 37 1/2" by 24"

$5,000-$6,500

Byrdcliffe Colony

Byrdcliffe Arts & Crafts Colony (1902-1910) founded by Ralph Radcliffe Whitehead and his wife, Jane Byrd McCall, in Woodstock, N.Y., produced furniture, pottery, textiles, metalwares.

Limbert double postcard desk

with letter slot divider holding a copper and brass cutout shade with owl motif on beige and ivory slag glass, with slatted partition and turned posts. (Originally made for the Yellowstone National Park hotel.) Refinished, new screws attaching shade, new sockets. Unsigned. 65 1/2" by 36" by 40"

$7,000-$9,000

Limbert Ebon-Oak single-drawer desk

and matching chair inlaid with small squares and lines of dark wood, and caned panels, the desk with open cubbies and letter holders. Desk refinished, some repairs to chips on front right, chair has excellent original finish. Branded mark. Desk: 35" by 36" by 20"

$1,900-$2,400/pair

Limbert partner's desk

No. 739, with central divider with pen tray and letter holders on either side, supported by trestle legs carved with a "B" and joined by a slatted keyed-through stretcher, accompanied by two chairs with arched and cut-out backs. Very good original finish, chairs overcoated but appear to have original upholstery. Branded mark. Desk: 42" by 36" by 36", chairs: 37 1/2" by 14 3/4" by 17"

$6,000-$7,000/set

Littles, Grand Rapids Furniture, postcard desk
with two drawers and a gallery top with a single drawer. Original finish, some looseness.
Paper label. 41" by 35 1/2" by 24 1/2"

$200-$300

Old Hickory single-drawer desk
with cantilevered sides and lower shelf with shaped back panel, accompanied by a
stool with woven split-cane seat. Original finish and reed, good condition. American
Provincial decal. Desk: 30" by 40" by 18 1/2", stool: 17 1/2" by 25" by 14 1/2"

$200-$300/pair

Onondaga Shops postcard desk
No. 404, with an arched kneehole opening. Original finish, one small drawer replaced,
split to one large drawer front. 35" by 40 1/4" by 23"

$850-$1,000

Rittencraft desk
with single drawer with copper drop pulls, and two open bookshelves to each side with
rectangular cut-out panels to front and back. Original finish, some looseness. Rittencraft
decal. 30" by 42" by 26"

$600-$700

Charles Rohlfs double pedestal desk

1902, with four drawers to one side and bookshelf/cabinet to the other, with strap hinges, rough-sawn panels, and carved R medallion. Complete with tall-back swiveling desk chair, carved with matching medallion and date, fleur-de-lys finial and tacked-on original red leather seat. Both pieces have an excellent original black finish with light overcoat, and original green interior. Missing support for cabinet shelf and several rivet heads, some wear around feet of chair. Carved CR/1902. Desk (on casters): 32 3/4" by 60" by 32 3/4", chair: 59" by 26" by 21"

$23,000-$28,000/pair

Gustav Stickley double-pedestal desk

with two banks of drawers to top, two pull-out shelves, and six drawers to bottom, all with hammered copper drop pulls. Restored original finish to base, refinished top, replaced hardware to small drawers. Red decal. 36 1/2" by 60" by 32"

$5,000-$6,000

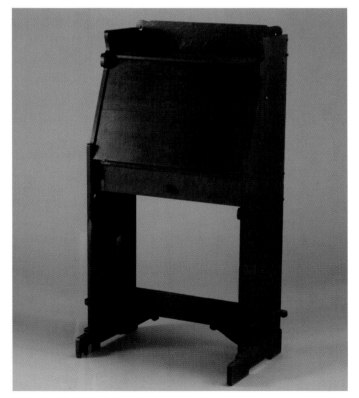

Charles Rohlfs chalet desk

1900, with gallery top and paneled back, drop-front with interior shelf and drawer, over single drawer with original green-finished interior, and carved stretcher keyed-through plank sides, with faceted nail heads. Excellent original finish, re-glued seam separation to door, some looseness to hinges. Red-stained signature, and 1900. 50 1/4" by 26" by 17"

$7,000-$8,000

Gustav Stickley desk

with raised two-door cabinet with interior shelves, and four drawers with faceted wooden pulls. Excellent original finish, one interior shelf missing, wear to kneehole edges from chair, seam separation and cupping to top and back panel. Large red decal. 47 1/4" by 36" by 22"

$6,500-$7,500

Gustav Stickley desk/bookcase

designed by Harvey Ellis, with a drop-front desk over two drawers and flanked by two bookcase doors with leaded glass panels, iron hardware. Original finish with original interior, including inkwells, intact, minor chip to top, a few chips repaired. Probably purchased from Gustav Stickley in 1903. 56" by 56" by 15"

$100,000+

Gustav Stickley double-pedestal desk

with paneled case, nine drawers with faceted wooden pulls, and lower shelf keyed through the sides. Refinished, tenons added, height added to legs, missing key, seam separations to top. Unmarked. 30" by 53 1/2" by 30"

$1,900-$2,200

Gustav Stickley drop-front desk

with five drawers, cast pulls, and gallery interior. Original finish, veneer on exterior of drop-front has been replaced, interior veneer repaired, minor edge wear. Branded mark. 45" by 36 1/2" by 15"

$3,000-$3,500

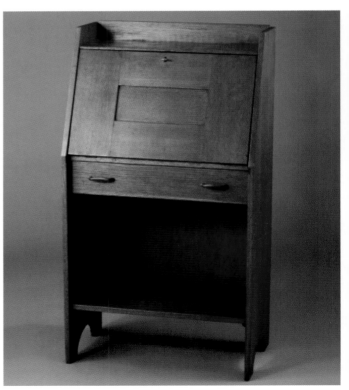

Gustav Stickley drop-front desk

with gallery top, paneled door over single drawer with cast bronze pulls, and lower shelf. Original finish, good condition. Large red decal. 47 1/4" by 25 3/4" by 15"

$3,500-$4,000

Gustav Stickley drop-front desk

with gallery top, paneled door and sides, two lower shelves, with key-lock and strap iron hardware. Murky original finish with color added, some chips and seam separation, re-glued break to one post, a little loose. Large decal. 52" by 26" by 11"

$3,000-$3,500

Gustav Stickley kneehole writing desk

with paneled sides and back, and five drawers with brass hardware. Refinished, separation to top. Unmarked. 28 1/2" by 42" by 24"

$1,500-$1,750

Gustav Stickley kneehole desk

with original tacked-on leather top, center drawer and recessed shelf, and two drawers to each side with hammered copper oval pulls. Original finish, supple leather, some tacks replaced, minor repairs to leather. Stamped mark, might not be original. 31" by 50" by 28"

$2,750-$3,250

Gustav Stickley mahogany desk

with overhanging top, paneled drop-front, and fitted interior with single drawer. Top refinished, color loss on bottom shelf, one mortise broken, some looseness, some missing screws. Red decal. 46 1/2" by 32" by 12"

$1,400-$1,800

Gustav Stickley mahogany drop-front desk
with gallery top, interior fittings and two-door cabinet below, with hammered copper strap hinges and V-pulls. Refinished, some edge roughness, repair to top of left door. Red decal. 51" by 25" by 31"

$4,000-$5,000

Gustav Stickley roll-top desk
No. 713, with interior gallery, locking center drawer and five additional drawers with iron oval pulls on tapering posts. Refinished, missing two interior brackets, replaced knobs to interior cubby drawers. Paper label. 46" by 60" by 32"

$5,000-$6,000

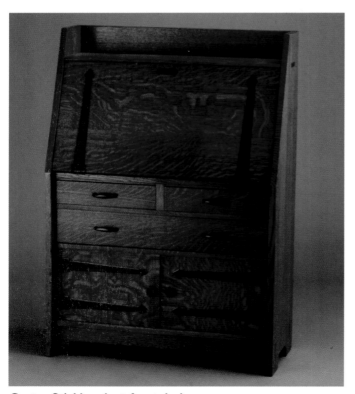

Gustav Stickley slant-front desk
with gallery top, three drawers and two cabinet doors, with strap hinges and hardware. Refinished and repatinated hardware. Red decal. 48" by 33" by 14"

$3,500-$4,000

Gustav Stickley postcard desk
with two letter holders, single drawer with circular wooden pulls, and tapering legs. Original finish, some wear to top, missing veneer on front leg, nine drill holes to center of gallery back. Branded mark. 35" by 28" by 18"

$1,100-$1,500

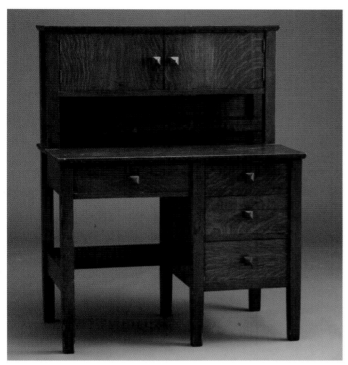

Gustav Stickley hutch-top postcard desk
1902-03, with four drawers below and two-door cabinet above, all with square wooden pulls, broad stretchers to one side, and paneled back, possibly a prototype or custom-ordered piece. Very good original finish and condition, separation to top surface, chip to inside of one leg. Large red decal. 47 1/2" by 36" by 22"

$13,000-$15,000

Gustav Stickley postcard desk
with two-letter backsplash, single drawer with hammered copper V-pull. Fine original finish. Branded mark. 33 1/4" by 32" by 20"

$3,500-$4,000

Gustav Stickley postcard desk
with letter holder backsplash, two drawers, paneled back and sides, and recessed bookshelf below. Original finish, some looseness, four screw holes in right side. Early red decal. 36" by 39 1/2" by 22"

$1,200-$1,600

Gustav Stickley roll-top desk
No. 619, with interior gallery, locking center drawer and five additional drawers with iron oval pulls on tapering posts. Refinished, replaced knobs to interior cubby drawers. Paper label. 46" by 48" by 32"

$2,800-$3,250

Gustav Stickley writing desk
circa 1904, oak, original finish and hardware, paper label and large red mark, 29" tall, 42" wide, 24" deep

$3,000-$3,400

L. & J.G. Stickley desk
with single blind drawer, and two bookshelves on either side with single slat to front and back. Refinished. Branded "The Work of..." 30" by 42" by 27 1/2"

$700-$800

L.& J.G. Stickley drop-front desk
with backsplash, interior gallery, six drawers with wooden pulls, and open bookshelf to each side. Original finish with overcoat, scratch to top. Unmarked. 41" by 45" by 21"

$1,600-$2,000

Stickley Bros. single-drawer desk
with slatted open bookshelves. Original finish, good condition. Quaint metal tag. 29" by 40" by 26"

$850-$950

Dressers

Limbert dresser
No. 479 1/2, two half drawers over two full drawers with original copper hardware, through-tenon construction, original swivel mirror, refinished, branded signature, 40" by 21" by 68"

$1,500-$1,800

Stickley Bros. dresser
No. 9015, two half drawers over three full drawers with original copper hardware, swivel plate glass mirror supported by original harp, fine original finish, signed with Quaint metal tag. 45" by 22" by 66"

$2,300-$2,800

Wolverine (Detroit) desk
with inset top, single drawer, and short slats to sides. Original finish, good condition. 29" by 43" by 27"

$600-$700

Onondaga Shops dresser
with two-over-four drawer configuration and brass-washed hammered copper pulls,
paneled sides and pivoting mirror. Some wear to original finish, separation and scratches
to top. Unmarked. 75" by 40" by 21 3/4"

$2,500-$3,000

Roycroft single-drawer dressing table
with integrated mirror, overhanging top and Mackmurdo feet. Excellent original finish
and condition, missing part of mirror hardware. Orb and cross mark. 56" by 39" by 17
1/2"

$6,000-$7,000

'Mackmurdo feet'

The design term
"Mackmurdo feet"—
which refers to an
abruptly tapering or
corseted leg with
an angular flared
foot—is in tribute
to Arthur Heygate
Mackmurdo (1851-
1942), a disciple of
John Ruskin and
William Morris. In
1882, Mackmurdo
founded the Century
Guild in England,
to produce work
with Arts & Crafts
designs.

Roycroft mahogany five-drawer dresser
with copper pulls and Mackmurdo feet. Original finish, missing mirror and harp, wear to drawer edges. Orb and cross
mark. 36" by 53 1/2" by 25 3/4"

$900-$1,100

Roycroft four-drawer dresser
with integrated mirror, brass pulls and Mackmurdo feet. Excellent original finish and condition. Orb and cross mark. 61 1/2" by 43 1/2" by 25 1/2"

$8,500-$10,000

Gustav Stickley four-drawer dresser
with hammered copper pulls and arched apron with attached pivoting mirror. Refinished, minor veneer chipping on sides. Red decal and paper label. 66" by 48" by 22"

$4,500-$5,000

L. & J.G. Stickley four-drawer dresser
No. 93, with mushroom pulls, arched apron, paneled sides and mirror. Original finish, wear and staining to top. Handcraft label. 69 1/4" by 48" by 22 1/4"

$2,000-$2,500

Stickley Bros. six-drawer dresser
with paneled sides, gallery top inlaid with Glasgow roses. Original finish, minor veneer chips from drawer fronts, missing key escutcheon, two pieces of metal inlay and bin pull from drawer hardware. 58" by 34" by 22"

$3,000-$3,500

Drink Stands

Gustav Stickley drink stand
No. 436, circular top over a stacked stretcher base with central facetted peg, double through-tenon construction at legs, refinished, unsigned, 24" by 28"

$3,000-$3,500

Splay-leg drink stand
in the style of Gustav Stickley, and of the period. Fine original finish.

$900-$1,200

L. & J.G. Stickley drink stand
circa 1912-15, oak, original finish, tongue in groove top, unmarked, 27" tall, 17" square

$1,200-$1,400

L. & J.G. Stickley drink stand
with square overhanging top, straight apron, and low stretchers. Original finish, minor loss to top, good condition. Unmarked. 28" by 15 1/2"

$600-$800

Stickley Bros. drink stand
with square inset top and three round-bottom slats to each side. Good original finish and condition. Paper label and stenciled number. 24 1/4" by 15" square

$1,000-$1,400

Footstools

Arts & Crafts footstool
possibly Stickley Bros., arched top with recovered leather, through-tenon construction at base, worn original finish, 20" by 14" by 16"

$275-$325

Lakeside Craft Shop footstool
(Sheboygan, Wis.) slatted form with through-tenon construction and original leatherette cover, original finish. 18" by 18" by 15"

$450-$550

Limbert "Cricket" footstool
No. 200, rectangular solid top with central cutout supported by flared slab legs, refinished, branded. 18" by 10" by 6"

$100-$150

Harden footstool
(Camden, N.Y.) with arched apron and slatted sides, with original drop-in leather seat. Original finish, some edge wear and glue drips. Unmarked. 16" by 20" by 14"

$650-$950

Harden footstool
(Camden, N.Y.) with slatted sides and arched apron with new tan leather drop-in seat. Original finish with old overcoat. Unmarked. 17 1/2" by 20" by 14 3/4"

$1,200-$1,600

Gustav Stickley footstool
No. 300, with tacked-on original brown leather seat, arched apron, and stretchers mortised through the posts. Original finish with very light overcoat, tears to leather. Red decal. 15 1/2" by 20" by 16"

$1,700-$2,000

L. & J.G. Stickley footstool
with spindled sides, arched apron, and tacked-on leather seat. Refinished, reupholstered in period leather. Unmarked. 17" by 18" by 13"

$1,200-$1,500

L. & J.G. Stickley footstool
with new tacked on-on leather over arched rails. Original finish, split to one post. Unsigned. 16" by 19" by 15"

$350-$450

L. & J.G. Stickley footstool
with tacked-on leather upholstery over arched aprons. Replaced upholstery, overcoated original finish. "The Work of..." decal. 18" by 12" by 15"

$400-$500

L. & J.G. Stickley footstool
with tacked-on brown leather top and arched sides. Original finish, new leather and tacks. "The Work of..." decal. 16" by 19 1/4" by 15 1/4"

$700-$800

L. & J.G. Stickley mahogany footstool
with replaced brown leather surface, arched apron and sides. Original finish, tacks applied to leg sides and tops. Unmarked. 16 1/4" by 19 1/4" by 15 1/2"

$400-$500

Stickley Bros. footstool
circa 1901-04, oak, original finish, leather and tacks, exaggerated Mackmurdo feet, unmarked. 18" by 20" by 14"

$800-$1,200

Gustav Stickley gout stool
No. 302, with four short flaring legs and rush seat. New finish and rush. Red decal. 12" square by 4 1/2"

$400-$500

Hall Trees

Limbert hall tree
No. 227, having original brass hooks at top over an umbrella holder with square cutouts and original drip pans, original finish, branded. 17" by 17" by 76"

$1,200-$1,500

Stickley Bros. hall tree
tapered form with through-tenon construction and original hooks over a copper drip pan, fine original finish, unsigned. 24" by 9" by 72"

$450-$525

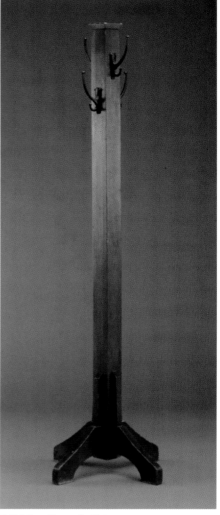

Hall Seat

Gustav Stickley hall seat
No. 224, paneled back over a lift seat compartment, slab sides with through-tenon construction and cutouts, recoated original finish, signed with red decal and remnant of paper label. 48" by 23" by 42"

$3,800-$4,300

Stickley Bros. hall tree
with tapering post, footed base, and four cast-iron double hooks. Good condition, original finish. Unmarked. 68" by 20" square

$700-$800

Floor Lamp

Gustav Stickley mahogany floor lamp
with silk-lined wicker shade, wrought iron hardware
and buttressed base. Original finish, drilled hole
on side, some breaks in shade, socket shaft broken.
Branded on bottom. 58" tall
$2,200-$2,800

Luggage Racks

Arts & Crafts luggage rack
manufactured by Grand Ledge (Mich.) Chair Co., in mahogany, slatted top
with applied brass tacks above tapered legs, original finish, some wear, signed
with paper label. 29" by 17" by 18"
$150-$200

Roycroft luggage rack
with paired keyed through stretchers. Overcoated original finish,
new screws under top. Carved orb and cross. 26" by 30" by 18"
$1,200-$1,600

Magazine Stands

Gustav Stickley magazine stand
No. 543, square top over four shelves with paneled side and through-tenon construction, original finish, branded signature, minor scratches. 16" by 16" by 44"

$1,800-$2,200

L. & J.G. Stickley magazine stand
No. 45, four shelves supported by arched sides and a paneled back over an arched toe board, fine original finish, signed "The work of..." 21" by 12" by 45"

$2,300-$2,600

Byrdcliffe Colony

Byrdcliffe Arts & Crafts Colony (1902-1910) founded by Ralph Radcliffe Whitehead and his wife, Jane Byrd McCall, in Woodstock, N.Y., produced furniture, pottery, textiles, metalwares.

Arts & Crafts magazine stand
the side panels with burnt-carved poppy design and four shelves with new tacked-on brown leather. Original finish, seam separation to one side. 44" by 20 1/2" by 10"
$650-$750

Byrdcliffe magazine stand
1904, with rectangular top, two lower shelves, and side panels carved with hollyhocks. Original finish, excellent condition. Branded mark. 35 3/4" by 14" by 11"
$12,000-$14,000

Byrdcliffe pagoda-shaped cherry magazine stand
with overhanging top, two shelves, and flaring sides painted with white lilies in opaque stain. Accompanied by the original drawing for the piece, marked Byrdcliffe/1904. Excellent condition, original finish to base, top refinished. 30" by 13" by 11"
$10,000-$14,000

Magazine stand
attributed to Lakeside Craft Shop (Sheboygan, Wis.)
with five stepped-back shelves. Unmarked. 40" by 16"
by 12"

$300-$400

Michigan Chair Co. magazine stand
with square cutouts along top, cutout sides, and three
graduated compartments. Original finish, repair to one
foot. Unmarked. 38" by 14" by 10 1/2"

$600-$700

**Michigan Chair Co. mahogany
magazine stand**
with overhanging rectangular top, four lower shelves,
slatted sides and flared legs. Original finish, top cleaned.
Remnant of paper label. 33 1/4" by 16 1/2"

$800-$1,000

Roycroft mahogany magazine stand
with three shelves and canted sides, arched top. Original finish, good condition, minor
edge wear. Orb and cross mark. 37 1/2" by 17 3/4" by 15 1/2"

$2,300-$2,800

Charles Stickley magazine stand
with tapered sides and four shelves. Good condition, overcoated original finish. Stickley
Brandt decal. 41 3/4" by 18 1/2" by 15"

$1,500-$1,700

Gustav Stickley magazine stand
with beveled top, paneled sides and four shelves.
Excellent original finish and condition, minor tack holes
and color loss to top corner. Full box decal. 43 3/4" by 15
1/4" by 15 1/4"

$3,000-$4,000

Gustav Stickley magazine stand
No. 514, with tongue-and-groove paneled sides, square
posts and leather strips tacked to shelf ends. Original
finish, wear to top. Early red decal under top shelf. 35
1/2" by 14 1/4" by 14 1/2"

$6,500-$8,000

Gustav Stickley magazine stand
with paneled sides and four shelves under an arched
apron. Refinished, missing tacks. Unmarked. 35 1/4" by
15" by 14 1/4"

$1,900-$2,400

Gustav Stickley magazine stand
with tapering posts, and gallery to each of the four shelves. Original finish, a trifle loose.
Red decal and partial paper label. 39" by 24 1/2" by 15"

$2,000-$2,400

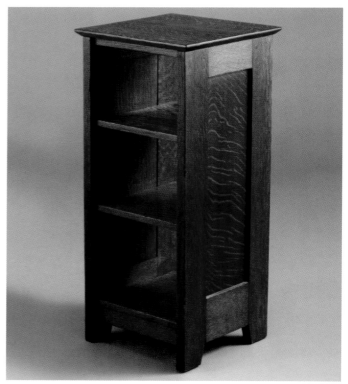

Gustav Stickley magazine stand
with beveled square top, paneled sides, and four shelves. Refinished, stains to top. Signed
under top. 35" by 15" square

$3,200-$3,800

Gustav Stickley Tree of Life magazine stand
with carved sides and four shelves. Original finish and tacks, minor edge wear. Unmarked. 43 1/2" by 14" square
$1,200-$1,600

Gustav Stickley Tree of Life magazine stand
with square overhanging top, flaring side panels with carved tree motif and four shelves. Original finish, a little loose, missing tacks and leather strips. Unmarked. 43 1/2" by 12 1/2" square
$1,600-$1,800

L. & J.G. Stickley magazine stand
with three vertical slats to each side, and four shelves. Excellent original finish. Co-joined label. 42" by 21" by 12"
$2,000-$2,25

L. & J.G. Stickley magazine stand
with three slats to each side, and four shelves. Skinned finish. "The Work of..." decal. 42" by 21" by 12"
$1,700-$2,000

L. & J.G. Stickley four-shelf magazine stand
with gallery top, paneled back, and arched stretchers. Original finish. Remnant of Handcraft decal. 45" by 19" by 12"
$2,300-$2,800

L. & J.G. Stickley slat-sided magazine stand
No. 46, with four shelves and arched top rails and apron. Original finish, excellent condition. Handcraft decal. 42 1/4" by 20" by 12"

$2,500-$3,500

L. & J.G. Stickley magazine stand
with slatted sides, curved stretchers, and four shelves. Original finish, minor edge roughness, some looseness. Unmarked. 42" by 21" by 12"

$1,200-$1,500

L. & J.G. Stickley/Onondaga Shops magazine stand
No. 346, with slatted sides and four shelves. Original finish, gouge to one side, a few minor ring stains. Unmarked. 42" by 21" by 12"

$850-$1,000

Stickley Bros. mahogany magazine rack
with gallery top, slatted back and sides, and five shelves. Refinished. Quaint metal tag. 46 1/2" by 15 1/4" by 12 1/2"

$800-$1,200

Stickley Bros. magazine stand
with gallery top, four shelves and slats to sides and back. Excellent original finish, minor scrapes to front. Stenciled number. 36" by 19" by 15"

$1,500-$2,000

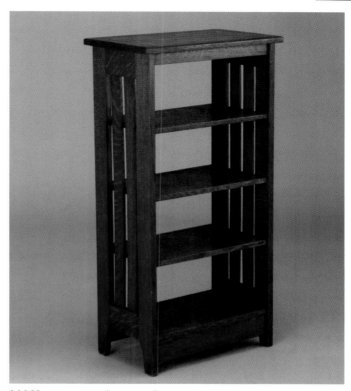

J.M. Young magazine stand
(Camden, N.Y., 1890-1979) with three shelves and slatted sides. Original finish with light overcoat, good condition. Paper label under top. 44" by 22" by 13 1/2"

$1,200-$1,600

Mantel

Arts & Crafts custom-designed oak mantel
with a carved Tree of Life flanked by stylized floral stained glass cupboard doors. Original finish, good condition. Unmarked. 82 1/2" by 59" by 14"

$3,300-$3,800

Mirrors

Arts & Crafts mirror
original beveled glass in hammered copper frame having pewter corners and a repousse floral decoration with enameled center, original patina. 30" by 25"

$1,200-$1,500

Arts & Crafts cheval mirror
central tilting mirror flanked by hinged mirrors at sides, shoe-foot base, refinished, minor roughness. Central frame 28" wide, side mirrors each 23" wide, overall height 72"

$1,000-$1,200

Limbert mirror
No. 21, original glass flanked by single slat and post with original copper hardware, original finish, branded and numbered. 36" by 27"

$800-$900

Charles Rohlfs hanging mirror
with original beveled glass and silver. Original finish, colored-in scratch, loss of silver. Branded mark. 38" by 28 1/2"

$650-$750

Cheval mirror
attributed to Stickley Bros., circa 1905-12, oak, original finish, glass and hardware. 67 1/2" tall, 27 1/2" wide

$3,500-$3,800

Roycroft hanging wall mirror
with broad mitered oak frame. Unmarked. 32 1/2" by 22"

$800-$1,000

L. & J.G. Stickley hanging mirror frame
with an overhanging top and arched apron. Original finish. Unmarked. 36" by 27 3/4"
$850-$1,150

Gustav Stickley pivoting dresser-top mirror
with inverted-V top rail and footed stand. Cleaned original finish, chip to edge. Branded mark. 21 1/2" by 23"
$1,000-$1,350

L. & J.G Stickley wall-hanging mirror
No.100, with arched top and recessed curve to bottom. Good original finish. "The Work of..." decal. 26 1/4" by 43"
$800-$1,000

Stickley Bros. hall mirror
with seven cast iron hooks and hanging hardware on mortised construction. Refinished, good condition. Paper label. 31 1/2" by 44"
$400-$500

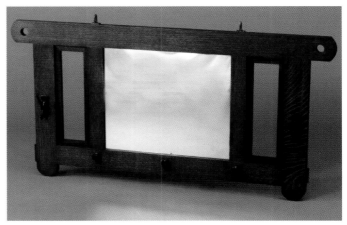

Hall mirror
attributed to Stickley Bros. with cut-out frame, two double iron hooks, two single chain hooks, and three single copper hooks. Refinished, decorative panels missing from either side of mirror, screw holes to bottom front. Unmarked. 28 1/4" by 53"
$500-$600

Nightstands

Arts & Crafts nightstand

trapezoidal form with open shelf over a single drawer with original wood knob, worn original finish. 21" by 14" by 29"

$450-$550

Gustav Stickley two-drawer nightstand
with backsplash, overhanging top, circular wooden pulls, and tapering legs. Good original finish to base, cleaned finish, screw hole and seam separation to top. Marked. 30 1/4" by 20" by 18"

$1,800-$2,200

Gustav Stickley "somno" (nightstand)
with single drawer, lower cabinet with paneled sides, and pyramidal wooden pulls. New finish. Unmarked. 33 1/2" by 19 3/4" by 16"

$3,800-$4,200

Pedestals
(also see Plant Stands)

Arts & Crafts pedestal
in mahogany, square top over an open compartment with elaborate design in copper trim, refinished. 13" by 13" by 40"

$1,100-$1,500

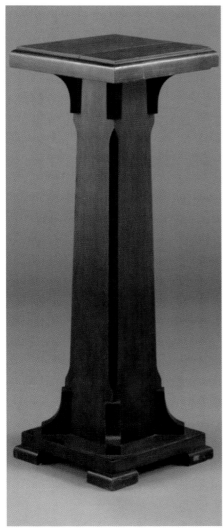

Arts & Crafts pedestal
with square top and four-sided base. Original finish, separation to top. 36" by 12" square

$600-$700

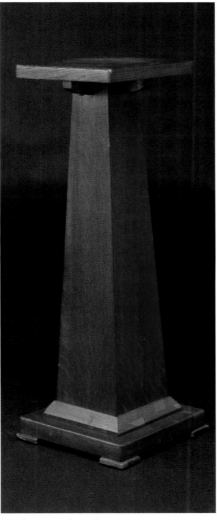

Limbert pedestal
with overhanging top on corbels and a stepped base. Original finish, normal wear to top, reglued at seam, minor chipping to feet. Branded mark. 32" by 12" square

$2,000-$2,500

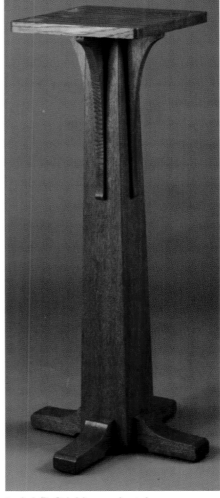

L. & J.G. Stickley pedestal
with square top supported by four long corbels, on a four-sided tapering post with shoe feet. Refinished top. Remnant of "The Work of..." decal, no. 28 in black marker. 42" by 18" square

$3,300-$3,800

Plant Stands

Lakeside Craft Shop plant stand
(Sheboygan, Wis.) circular top with an inset hammered brass bowl supported by three legs with a pierced cutout design, original finish. 13" by 13" by 23"

$650-$750

Limbert plant stand
hexagonal top over a tapered six-sided base, original finish, branded signature. 13" by 13" by 37"

$500-$600

Prairie School plant stand
in walnut, square top over an arched through-tenon stretcher on a cruciform base, refinished, some restoration. 15" by 15" by 31"

$250-$300

Gustav Stickley plant stand
No. 41, early form, square top over notched apron and vertical lower stretcher with keyed-tenon construction, refinished, unsigned. 14" square by 28"

$1,000-$1,500

Stickley Brothers plant stand
No. 133, mahogany, square top above a tapered base, original finish, signed with Quaint metal tag. 13" by 13" by 34"

$800-$1,000

Limbert plant stand
with quarter-round corbels under the square top, flaring sides with ovoid cutouts, lower shelf, and plank base. Fine original finish, factory edge repair to top and seam separation to side. No visible mark. 29 1/2" by 20" square

$5,000-$7,000

Prairie School

The Prairie School of design derived from the publication in 1901 of "A Home in a Prairie Town," which architect Frank Lloyd Wright designed for the Ladies' Home Journal. Design themes included horizontal forms and abstract geometric elements.

Roycroft plant stand
with tapering posts and panel sides. New dark finish. Carved orb and cross mark. 28" by 13 1/2" square

$2,200-$2,800

Gustav Stickley plant stand
with square top, arched apron, and H-shaped keyed-through stretcher. Refinished, separation to top. 1902 decal. 25 1/2" by 14" square

$1,500-$2,000

Gustav Stickley plant stand
with keyed through-tenon stretcher and inset Grueby square tile top. Restored original finish, excellent condition, small chip to edge of regrouted tile. Red decal. 26" by 14" square

$8,000-$10,000

Gustav Stickley plant stand
with four tapering legs. Red decal. 28 1/2" by 12"

$750-$850

Gustav Stickley plant stand
with square top flush with cloud-lift apron, over narrow board mortised through corseted stretchers with tenon and key. Original finish, crack to one stretcher, finishing nail in top. 1902-04 Red decal. 27" by 14" square

$2,800-$3,200

Stickley Bros. pedestal plant stand
with square top and base on pyramidal feet. Original finish to base, top refinished. Quaint metal tag with stenciled number. 34" by 13" square

$1,500-$2,000

L. & J.G. Stickley plant stand
good original finish and condition. Handcraft decal. 28" by 13 1/2" by 13 1/2"

$1,400-$1,600

Gustav Stickley plant stand
No. 660, with square, clip-corner top and broad apron, on flaring legs. Refinished. Craftsman paper label. 20 1/4" by 17" square

$850-$1,250

Plate Rack

Gustav Stickley hanging plate rack
with plate rail, lower shelf and chamfered back. Skinned medium brown finish. Unmarked. 28" by 46 1/2"

$2,000-$3,000

Porch Glider

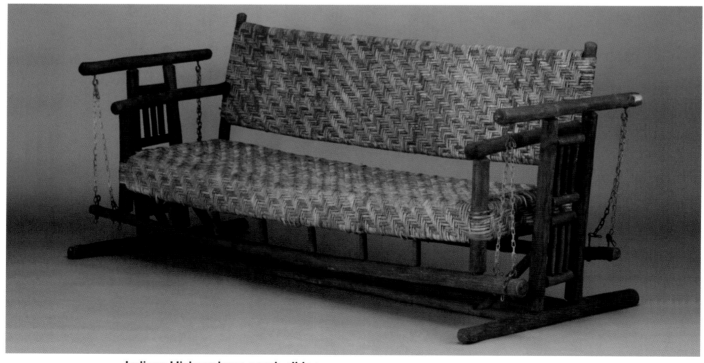

Indiana Hickory large porch glider
with original split reed seat and back. Some graying to hickory. Branded signature.

$3,200-$3,800

Screens

Stickley Bros. screen

No. 7580, three-panel form, each section consisting of three vertical slats over a leather insert, original finish, replaced leather. Each section is 20" wide, 66" tall

$1,500-$1,800

Arts & Crafts three-panel folding screen

with hand-printed fabric on both sides depicting a castle among hills and trees in browns, blues, and greens. Original finish. Unmarked. 63 3/4" by 57 1/4"

$400-$500

Gustav Stickley three-fold paneled oak screen

with green leather inserts to top. Refinished (skinned and oiled), with some chips to wood, replaced leather. Unmarked. Each panel: 68 3/4" by 22 1/4"

$2,500-$3,000

Gustav Stickley three-panel room screen

each section with square leather top panel and five cutout vertical slats below. Coarse new finish, missing hinge pins, restoration to original leather panels. Black decal. 69 3/4" tall

$5,000-$6,000

Secretary

Arts & Crafts secretary/bookcase

with overhanging rectangular top, full gallery interior over single drawer and bottom shelf, flanked by two glass-paned doors with mullion latticework, and interior shelves. Overcoated original finish, delamination to back. Unmarked. 50" by 62 1/2" by 14"

$1,800-$2,200

Servers

L. & J.G. Stickley server

No. 751, rectangular top over a single blind drawer, shortened, nicely refinished, signed with conjoined decal. 32" by 18" by 32"

$650-$750

Arts & Crafts server

with arched cut-out backsplash with single drawer and lower shelf. Original finish, minor seam separation on top. 37" by 36" by 19"

$200-$300

Limbert server

with reticulated backsplash, two drawers with square hammered copper pulls, and two lower shelves. Excellent original finish and condition. Branded mark. 43 1/4" by 40" by 19"

$2,200-$2,800

Limbert trapezoidal server

with single drawer, arched apron and sides, and recessed lower shelf mortised through the legs. Original finish. Branded mark. 29" by 60" by 18"

$8,000-$10,000

Server

with mirrored backsplash, possibly Lifetime, with open shelf to each side and two drawers with square copper pulls, on casters. Original finish. Number 1214. 44" by 54" by 20"

$500-$600

Charles Stickley two-drawer server
with backsplash, overhanging rectangular top, and brass pulls. Original finish, minor seam separation, some looseness. Signed Charles Stickley. 35" by 42 1/2" by 20"
$1,200-$1,700

Gustav Stickley server
with backsplash, three drawers with hammered copper oval pulls, and a lower shelf. Skinned original finish. Red decal. 39" by 48" by 19 3/4"
$3,500-$4,500

Gustav Stickley server
with a plate rail and two drawers over one long drawer, oval pulls. Original finish, good condition. Red decal inside right drawer. 44" by 48" by 21"
$3,000-$3,500

Gustav Stickley server
with backsplash, four-drawers with hammered copper oval pulls, and lower shelf. Original finish, minor stains to top. Red decal and paper label. 38" by 48" by 20"
$3,200-$3,800

Gustav Stickley server

with backsplash, three small drawers over one large, all with riveted hammered copper oval pulls, and lower shelf. Refinished, patina loss to hardware. Marked. 39 1/4" by 48" by 19 3/4"

$2,400-$2,800

Gustav Stickley server

with plate rail, through-tenon construction with paneled back and sides, and two drawers over a lower shelf and linen drawer, with pyramidal wooden pulls. Very good original finish, normal wear from normal use, a few gouges on plate rail. Rare form. Large red decal. 44 1/4" by 59" by 29"

$33,000-$38,000

Gustav Stickley two-drawer server

designed by Harvey Ellis with backsplash, riveted iron pulls, and arched apron, with lower shelf. Skinned original finish. Red decal. 40" by 42" by 18"

$3,500-$4,000

Gustav Stickley server

with backsplash, three small drawers over a linen drawer, all with riveted hammered copper oval pulls, and lower shelf. Original finish, some unevenness. Red decal. 39 1/4" by 48" by 20"

$3,000-$4,000

Stickley Bros. server

with backsplash, single drawer with hammered brass hardware and lower shelf. Good original finish, light wear to edges of legs, some light staining to top. Branded Stickley Brothers, stenciled B735. 37" by 36" by 19"

$1,500-$2,000

Settees

L. & J.G. Stickley settee

No. 214, Prairie School influence with twenty-two curved slats at back and six under each arm, through-tenon construction, recovered original cushion, fine original finish, branded "The Work of ..." 60" by 21" by 33"

$5,000-$6,000

Gustav Stickley settee

No. 165, with tapering pyramidal posts, arched vertical back slats and cloud lift stretcher. Includes leather cushion. Refinished, good condition. 40 1/2" by 59 1/2" by 28"

$5,000-$6,000

Gustav Stickley cube settee

1902-03, with horizontal slats, the top one mortised through the front legs, and three loose cushions re-upholstered in red vinyl (not shown). Excellent condition with thin overcoat to finish, tack holes on top of back rail. Stickley box mark. 27" by 78" by 33"

$6,000-$7,000

Settles

Limbert settle
No. 558 3/4, even-arm form with three vertical slats on each end and nine slats at back, recovered cushions in brown leather, refinished, signed and numbered. 86" by 32" by 38"
$4,000-$4,500

Limbert settle
No. 649, fourteen slats to back, single flared slat under each arm with spade cutout, original drop-in seat and back cushions, original finish, branded, paper label. 78" by 27" by 40"
$2,500-$3,000

Shop of the Crafters settle
(Cincinnati, Ohio, active 1904-20) even arm form with eight flared slats at back and two under each arm, peaked top rail has cutout design that is repeated on two lower slats, fine original finish, unsigned. 77" by 30" by 37"
$1,900-$2,300

Gustav Stickley settle
No. 219, in mahogany, drop arm form with seventeen slats to back, replaced cane foundation, replaced cushion in brown leather, lightly recoated original finish, red decal. 72" by 28" by 38"
$1,900-$2,200

L. & J.G. Stickley settle
No. 222, even-arm form with five slats to sides and twenty slats to back, original leather cushion and two original leather pillows, fine original finish, a couple tears to the leather cushion, signed "The Work of..." 76" by 31" by 39"
$8,000-$10,000

Stickley Bros. settle
No. 3504, drop arm form with 12 vertical slats at back, replaced drop-in cushion, worn original finish, some roughness to arms. 50" by 21" by 38"
$400-$600

Stickley Bros. settle
No. 3863, even-arm form with 19 shaped slats at back and eight under each side, through tenon construction, original finish with some restoration. 61" by 30" by 36"
$4,000-$5,000

Arts & Crafts even-arm settle
with spindles and slats to back and sides, and striped fabric-upholstered spring seat cushion. Refinished, new corner blocks, metal braces added between stretchers and legs. Unmarked. 33" by 82" by 29"
$1,800-$2,300

Karpen cube settle
(Chicago, active 1880 to 1952) with broad vertical slats to back and arms, with fabric upholstered cushion. Original finish, metal brackets added under seat for support. Metal tag. 36" by 76" by 25"
$2,300-$2,800

Lifetime drop-arm settle
(Hastings, Mich., active 1911-20) with seven broad back slats and two under each flat arm. Replaced fabric cushion, refinished, repair to slat under arm. Partial paper label. 39 3/4" by 74 1/4" by 29"
$1,200-$1,50

Limbert drop-arm settle
with vertical slats to back and sides, with black leather drop-in seat cushion. Refinished. Branded mark. 39 1/4" by 80" by 29 3/4"
$1,800-$2,200

Shop of the Crafters cube settle

(Cincinnati, Ohio, active 1904-20) designed by Paul Horti for the Crafters Library Set, 1906, with post of exotic wood inlay capped with tacked-on hammered metal fittings, vertical slats to the back, slatted cross work under the arms, with upholstered cordovan leather cushions. (Only six examples known.) Very good original finish. Original paper label. 37" by 67" by 30 1/2"

$12,000-$15,000

Charles Stickley settle

with vertical back slats and drop-in seat, on casters. Worn original finish, seam separations to posts. Branded. 36 1/2" by 76" by 31 1/2"

$2,800-$3,300

Charles Stickley settle

with heavy square posts, slats to back and sides under a rounded rail, and new tan leather drop-in seat and two loose cushions. Cleaned original finish, two rub spots inside center back slats. Branded center back stretcher. 31" by 76" by 31 1/2"

$4,000-$4,800

Gustav Stickley crib settle

with square posts, angled vertical slats to back and sides, and new rope seat support. New dark finish and corner blocks on underside, no cushion. Unmarked. 39" by 68 1/2" by 33"

$4,500-$5,000

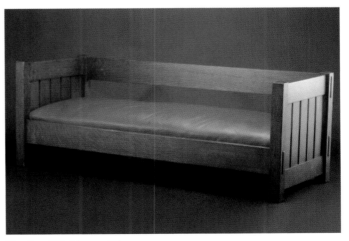

Gustav Stickley settle

with broad backrail and vertical slats to sides, re-upholstered in brown leather. Refinished, good condition. Branded mark. 29" by 78" by 31"

$5,500-$6,500

Gustav Stickley settle

No. 222, with tapering posts, tightly spaced canted slats to back and sides, and vinyl-upholstered drop-in seat. Fine original finish and condition, minor veneer chips and lifting on legs. Red decal. 36" by 80" by 32"

$9,000-$12,000

L. & J.G. Stickley tall-back settle

with open arms, vertical back slats, and slats to the floor from the seat rail, with drop-in seat cushion. Refinished and reupholstered, roughness to front legs. "The Work of..." label. 45" by 58" by 23"

$3,250-$3,750

L. & J.G. Stickley even-arm settle

No. 232, with horizontal back slats, broad vertical slats to sides and drop-in cushion with replaced leather. Original finish, very good condition. Unsigned. 32 1/2" by 72" by 24"

$2,500-$3,000

L. & J.G. Stickley even-arm settle

No. 281, with vertical slats, pyramidal posts and fabric-upholstered drop-in seat. Cleaned original finish, good condition. Unmarked. 34" by 76" by 31"

$6,000-$7,000

L. & J.G. Stickley even-arm settle

with broad vertical slats and drop-in seat cushion. Original finish and leather (leather very good but rips to sides). Unsigned. 28" by 71" by 27"

$2,500-$3,000

J.M. Young drop-arm settle

(Camden, N.Y., active 1890 to 1979) with vertical slats on back and under paddle arms. Original finish, missing drop-in seat, supports for seat have been moved, crossbar and screw caps missing, scuffs and edge wear to back. 34 1/4" by 81 1/2" by 31 1/2"

$1,200-$1,600

Sewing Stand

Roycroft mahogany sewing stand

with three center drawers with round wooden pulls, flanked by lift-top storage compartments, on tapering legs. Fine new finish. Carved orb and cross mark. 29" by 29 3/4" by 16 1/2"

$3,000-$3,500

Sideboards

Arts & Crafts sideboard

by Henshaw Furniture Co., Cincinnati, Ohio, mirrored back with keyed-tenon construction above a base cabinet with Mackmurdo feet and a series of drawers with sculpted handles and cabinet doors, recoated original finish, signed with paper label, one handle broken. 60" by 24" by 58"

$800-$1,000

Gustav Stickley sideboard

No. 814 1/2, three half drawers flanked by cabinet doors with strap hinges over a full drawer, original copper hardware, refinished with some restoration, branded signature. 56" by 22" by 49"

$2,500-$3,000

Gustav Stickley sideboard

No. 816, original plate rail over a full drawer and three half drawers flanked by two cabinet doors, original iron hardware, original finish, signed with red decal. 48" by 19" by 45"

$3,000-$4000

Arts & Crafts sideboard

with mirrored backsplash and plate shelf, over two drawers, a linen drawer and three cabinets, two with green slag glass panels. Original finish, stains and splits to top, some warping and looseness, replaced glass, some screws missing from hardware. 58" by 50" by 24"

$550-$650

Arts & Crafts sideboard

with clip-corner mirror backsplash, four drawers and two cabinets with copper strap hardware. Refinished, missing one escutcheon plate. 58" by 54" by 22"

$200-$300

Arts & Crafts sideboard

with beveled mirror backsplash, four drawers and two cabinets on casters. Original finish with overcoat, good condition. 55 1/2" by 61 1/2" by 25"

$800-$1,200

'Mackmurdo feet'

The design term "Mackmurdo feet"—which refers to an abruptly tapering or corseted leg with an angular flared foot—is in tribute to Arthur Heygate Mackmurdo (1851-1942), a disciple of John Ruskin and William Morris. In 1882, Mackmurdo founded the Century Guild in England, to produce work with Arts & Crafts designs.

English Arts & Crafts sideboard
with corniced open top, mirror and two small cabinets with bull's-eye-glass panes, with five-drawers and the cabinets below. Good condition. 76 1/2" by 61" by 24"

$1,500-$2,000

Limbert sideboard
with two glass-paned cabinets flanking a central mirrored backsplash with shelf, and five drawers surrounding a protruding two-door cabinet, all with angular brass drop pulls. Overcoated original finish but overall good condition, missing escutcheons and one glass pane. Paper label. On casters: 60 1/2" by 60" by 21"

$7,000-$8,000

Limbert sideboard
with mirrored backsplash, two small drawers and cabinets over a linen drawer. Original finish, staining to top. Branded in drawer. 53 1/2" by 60" by 21 1/4"

$1,500-$2,000

Charles Rohlfs mahogany sideboard
with five drawers flanked on either side by a small drawer over cabinet, with faceted from legs and pulls. Refinished top, some replaced hardware, screw holes inside both doors. Branded mark. 41 1/4" by 68 3/4" by 22 1/4"

$4,000-$4,500

Roycroft sideboard

with mirrored backsplash, a central drawer over two shelves, flanked on either side by a drawer and cabinet, with copper strap hinges and Mackmurdo feet. Overcoated original medium finish, good condition. Carved "Roycroft." 64 1/2" by 62 1/4" by 28"

$15,000-$17,000

Shop of the Crafters sideboard

(Cincinnati, Ohio, active 1904-20) with rounded, mirrored backsplash, linen drawer over three small drawers and two cabinet doors with stylized floral inlay, all with oval copper pulls. Refinished, good condition. Paper label. 56 3/4" by 53 1/2" by 25"

$6,000-$7,000

Shop of the Crafters sideboard

(Cincinnati, Ohio, active 1904-20) with arched mirror backsplash over four drawers with hammered copper pulls, two cabinet doors inlaid with stylized floral motif, and an open cabinet, on casters. Good original finish, scratch to top. Paper label. 58" by 54" by 25"

$4,000-$4,500

Gustav Stickley eight-leg sideboard

circa 1901-04, oak, refinished, original hammered-iron strap hinges and pulls, unmarked, 50" tall (after 1904, this form was slightly shorter). 70" wide, 26" deep

$8,500-$9,500

Gustav Stickley eight-leg sideboard
with paneled back, plate rail, and four center drawers flanked on either side by a cabinet with interior shelves, riveted hammered copper strap hinges and drop pulls. Refinished, patina loss to hardware. Unmarked. 50" by 70" by 25 1/2"

$5,500-$6,500

Gustav Stickley eight-legged sideboard
circa 1902, with chamfered backsplash, four drawers and two doors with extremely rare copper hardware. Excellent original finish with only minor staining to top, small chip to leg, repair to three small drill holes, restoration to copper patina. '02-'03 decal on back. 49 1/2" by 70" by 25"

$15,000-$17,000

Gustav Stickley sideboard
1902-03, with gallery top, two drawers with iron hardware pulls over two cabinet doors with butterfly joints, and keyed through-tenon sides. Refinished, new keys on both sides, braces added to backside of doors. Eastwood paper label. 42 1/2" by 50" by 23"

$10,000-$14,000

Gustav Stickley sideboard
No. 814, with plate rail, two doors with strap hinges, three center drawers and a linen drawer with hammered copper V-pulls. Cleaned original finish, minor veneer lifting, screw hole to plate rail. Red decal. 48" by 66" by 24"

$6,000-$7,000

Gustav Stickley sideboard
No. 814, with plate rail, three center drawers and two cabinets over a linen drawer, with hammered copper hardware and strap hinges. Refinished, veneer lifting on doors, separations to top, cleaned patina to hardware. Craftsman paper label. 48 3/4" by 56" by 22"

$2,500-$3,000

Gustav Stickley sideboard
No. 814 1/2, with plate rail, two doors with strap hinges, three center drawers and a linen drawer with hammered copper V-pulls. Refinished, veneer lifting on side panels and doors. Red decal and paper label. 48 1/2" by 55 1/2" by 22"

$4,500-$5,500

Gustav Stickley sideboard
with plate rail, linen drawer over two cabinets and three center drawers, with arched apron. Cleaned original finish, a couple of small chips and veneer lifting. Decal and paper label. 45" by 48" by 18"

$3,000-$3,750

Gustav Stickley sideboard
designed by Harvey Ellis, with backsplash and plate rest over six drawers with hammered copper pulls, an arched apron, and lower shelf. Original finish, replaced back paneling, minor nicks to legs. Red decal. 42" by 54" by 21"

$9,000-$12,000

Gustav Stickley sideboard
with plate rail, two cabinets and three drawers over linen drawer, all with hammered copper hardware. Refinished, veneer damage on left side, some edge roughness. Craftsman paper label. 47 1/2" by 66" by 23 3/4"

$3,800-$4,200

Gustav Stickley sideboard
with plate rail with arched top, two cabinets with hammered copper strap hinges and hardware flanking three center drawers over a linen drawer. Refinished. Branded mark. 48" by 56" by 22"

$3,000-$3,750

L. & J.G. Stickley sideboard

with paneled plate rack over five drawers and two doors with coarsely repatinated hardware. Original finish with overcoat. "The Work of..." decal. 48" by 66" by 22"

$2,500-$3,000

Stickley Bros. sideboard

with paneled plate rack, four drawers and three panel doors with hammered brass hardware. Good original finish, wear to copper patina on iron hardware, wear around feet. Branded Stickley Brothers, stenciled 8833 1/2. 45" by 56" by 22"

$3,000-$3,800

Stickley Bros. sideboard

with paneled plate rail, two drawers over one with brass-washed hammered copper pulls, and two cabinets. Original finish, wear spot with color added to top. Branded mark. 46" by 50" by 22"

$1,900-$2,400

L. & J.G. Stickley sideboard

with plate rail backsplash, four center drawers and two paneled cabinet doors with strap hardware and copper pulls over a linen drawer. Original finish, some wear to top, a few chips to front edge. Handcraft decal. 48 1/2" by 54" by 25"

$5,000-$6,000

L. & J.G. Stickley/Onondaga Shops sideboard

No. 737, with plate shelf over mirrored backsplash, two paneled cabinet doors with strap hinges flanking four center drawers, all over a linen drawer. Good original finish. Unmarked. 62" by 54" by 24"

$4,000-$5,000

Stickley Bros. sideboard

with mirrored backsplash, four drawers and two doors with hammered copper strap hinges and pulls. Good original finish, back is delaminating. Quaint metal tag. 48" by 54" by 21"

$1,800-$2,300

Stickley Bros. sideboard

No. 8216, with paneled plate rail, linen drawer over three center drawers flanked by two paneled-door cabinets, all with brass-washed, hammered copper hardware. Refinished. Stenciled number. 44 1/4" by 54 1/4" by 21"

$3,000-$3,500

Sideboard

attributed to Stickley Bros. with mirrored backsplash, two-over-one drawer configuration and three paneled cabinet doors with circular wooden pulls, on Mackmurdo-style feet. Original finish, one replaced knob. Obscured stenciled number. 51 1/2" by 53 1/2" by 22"

$1,000-$1,400

Sofa

Scottish baronial-style three-seat sofa
with repousse backplates and corner brackets depicting a hunt scene with flowers and fruit, arched panels to sides. Refinished, break to right leg under metal, some veneer missing from top, some separations. Unmarked. 43" by 74" by 25"

$2,200-$2,500

Stools

Limbert telephone stool
No. 061, plank seat over arched rail with bow tie slat at back, refinished, branded, minor repairs. 12" by 14" by 24"

$125-$175

Limbert stool
with tacked-on brown canvas upholstery, single drawer with square hammered copper pulls and escutcheon, arched apron and sides. Some wear to original finish, upholstery possibly original, some paint splatters. Branded mark. 12 3/4" by 18" by 12"

$1,000-$1,300

Scottish baronial-style cube stool
with repousse hammered-copper panel and rivets to apron and legs, depicting exotic birds and flowers, and keyhole-shaped legs. Refinished top, some damage to metal, missing glue blocks, veneer chips. Unmarked. 16 3/4" by 16 1/2" square

$700-$800

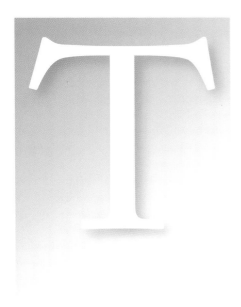

Tables, Console

Limbert console table
with trestle legs and three central slats over one long stretcher. Refinished, very good condition. Branded under top. 29" by 72" by 22"

$4,000-$5,000

Stickley Bros. console table
with six barley-twist legs, cross stretchers and bracketed aprons on bun feet. Original finish, wear to top, excellent condition. Branded, partial paper label. 31" by 72" by 32"

$1,200-$1,500

Tables, Dining

Arts & Crafts dining table
circular top over an octagonal pedestal base with support columns and extended feet, four leaves, cleaned original finish, burn to top. 48" diameter by 30"

$550-$650

Limbert dining table
square top with five original leaves supported by a tapered pedestal base, refinished, branded signature, square dining tables are very difficult to find. 41" by 35" by 29"

$2,500-$3,000

Gustav Stickley dining table
no. 632, circular top and apron over five tapered legs, four original 11" leaves, original finish, signed with red decal. 54" diameter by 29"

$4,000-$4,500

Arts & Crafts extension dining table
with shoe feet and two leaves. Labeled Corey David, Shelbeyville, Ind. 28 1/2" by 48" diameter

$900-$1,000

Arts & Crafts extension dining table
with circular top and octagonal pedestal base with four flaring buttressed feet. Includes one new 12" leaf. Overcoated original finish. Unmarked. Closed: 28 3/4" by 48" diameter

$450-$550

Lifetime Puritan Line five-leg extension dining table
with three leaves. Original finish, minor stain to top. Paper label under top. 28 3/4" by 54" diameter

$1,500-$1,800

Charles Rohlfs mahogany single-pedestal extension dining table
with circular top and cut-out trestle legs. Includes four 13 1/4" leaves. New finish, good condition. Carved CR/1902. Closed: approx. 35" by 54" diameter

$6,000-$7,000

Roycroft mahogany extension dining table
circular top with broad apron, on four legs with shoe feet. Refinished, base shows repair where it meets top, scratches to top, no leaves. Carved orb and cross mark. On casters: 29 1/2" by 60"

$5,000-$6,000

Gustav Stickley experimental circular dining table
with cross-stretchers mortised through the tapering plank legs. Base has original finish, top is refinished, separation to boards on top. Unmarked. 30" by 60" diameter

$3,000-$3,800

Gustav Stickley five-leg extension dining table
with overhanging circular top and four 12" leaves. Refinished, good condition. Paper label. 29" by 48" diameter

$3,500-$4,000

Gustav Stickley five-leg extension dining table
with four leaves. Restored finish on base, top refinished, two panels of apron veneer replaced. Paper label. 29" by 54" diameter

$4,500-$5,500

Gustav Stickley five-leg extension dining table
with two leaves. Overcoated original finish on base, top refinished, veneer repair to apron. Paper label. 28 1/2" by 48" diameter

$2,000-$2,500

Gustav Stickley split-pedestal dining table
No. 656, with five leaves. Refinished, good condition, veneer chips to skirt and base. Shadow of a decal on pedestal side. 29" by 60" diameter

$4,000-$5,000

L. & J.G. Stickley five-leg extension dining table
with circular top. Original finish to base, refinished top, some roughness to legs. Branded "The Work of..." On risers (one missing). Closed: 30 1/2" by 48" diameter

$2,000-$2,500

L. & J.G. Stickley extension dining table
with circular top, pedestal base and shoe feet, complete with four leaves. Original finish, some stains to top. Unmarked. Closed: 30" by 48" diameter

$3,500-$4,000

L. & J.G. Stickley dining table
with circular top, serpentine apron, and cross-stretchers keyed-through shaped plank legs, topped by a wooden finial. Original finish to base, refinished top, excellent condition. "The Work of..." tag. 30" by 72" diameter

$10,000-$12,000

Stickley Bros. circular extension dining table
on octagonal pedestal base with scrolled feet, complete with a rack of four leaves. Good original finish, cleaned top, some wear to feet. Paper label. 29 1/2" by 54" diameter

$2,000-$3,000

Stickley Bros. extension dining table
No. 2424, with circular top and apron over cross-stretchers with pyramidal block finial. Includes three later 8" leaves and custom-made table pad. Recent dark finish. Paper label. Closed (on casters): 30" by 48" diameter

$2,400-$3,000

Stickley Bros. extension dining table
with circular top and flaring, faceted pedestal with shoe feet, includes four 12" leaves. Original finish with overcoat, good condition. Remnants of stenciled model number. Closed (on casters): 31 1/2" by 48" diameter

$1,800-$2,300

Stickley Bros. Quaint round dining room table
circa 1912-15, oak, original finish, solid pedestal, four 12" leaves, block skirt, uncommon form. 60" diameter

$6,500-$6,800

Stickley Bros. split-pedestal extension dining table
No. 2428, with shoe feet and two additional leaves. Refinished. Quaint metal tag. 29 1/2" by 48" diameter

$2,000-$2,500

Tables, Drop-Leaf

Stickley Bros. drop-leaf table
No. 2817, with a fine original finish, signed with branded signature. Closed: 30" by 14" by 27"

$1,200-$1,500

Limbert gate-leg drop-leaf extension dining table
No.1148, with oval top and arched sides. Includes two leaves. Original finish, slight staining to top. Unmarked. Open: 29 1/2" by 42" by 64"

$1,400-$1,800

Old Hickory drop-leaf table
with circular top over spindled legs. Top refinished, very good condition. Branded mark under top. 29" by 36" diameter

$700-$900

L. & J.G. Stickley small drop-leaf table
circa 1910, with a square top, cut-out plank legs and shoe feet. Excellent original finish and condition. "The Work of..." decal. Open: 24" by 24" square

$4,500-$5,000

L. & J.G. Stickley drop-leaf gate-leg table
with shoe feet. Refinished. Branded "The Work of..." Open: 30" by 41 1/2" diameter

$1,500-$1,900

L. & J.G. Stickley drop-leaf table
with circular top and arched cross-stretchers. Original medium-dark finish, replaced table supports, staining and finish loss to top. Handcraft decal. Open: 29" by 35 1/2" diameter

$750-$1,000

Tables, Lamp

Limbert lamp table
No. 148, circular top over a vertical wide lower stretcher with rectangular cutouts, branded signature, refinished, 30" by 29"

$2,700-$3,200

Arts & Crafts circular lamp table
possibly Stickley, with overhanging top, arched cross stretchers and circular lower shelf. Top has overcoated original finish, base is refinished. 29" by 24" diameter

$800-$900

Arts & Crafts hexagonal parlor or lamp table
in the style of Gustav Stickley, original leather top and tacks, stacked stretchers with keyed tenons, burnt-carved Glasgow rose decoration on legs, original worn surface, unmarked. 29" by 30" diameter

$3,500

Berkey & Gay lamp table
(Grand Rapids, Mich., active 1873 to late 1920s) with circular top incorporating seven butterfly keys, on faceted legs with cross-stretchers. Refinished, a little loose. Branded circular mark. 29 3/4" by 30" diameter

$1,000-$1,200

Limbert lamp table
circa 1906-09, oak, original finish, cutout stretchers, top with tongue-in-groove construction (also found with spline construction), Grand Rapids and Holland mark. 30" by 30" diameter

$4,000-$4,200

Limbert lamp table
with square cut-outs, rectangular top and vertical stretcher mortised through the sides. New finish. Unmarked. 27" by 30" by 24"

$4,000-$4,500

Limbert lamp table
with circular top and broad cross-stretchers with square cut-outs. Refinished. Branded mark. 28" by 30" diameter

$1,500-$2,000

Onondaga Shops lamp table
with circular overhanging top and circular bottom shelf. Refinished, some of the seams have been rejoined and the top reglued. Onondaga Shops decal. 28" by 24"

$1,000-$1,500

Charles Rohlfs lamp table
with octagonal top, two lower shelves mortised through cut-out legs and fastened with long keyed-through tenons. Refinished, some stains to top. Branded mark. 29" by 26"

$6,500-$7,500

Gustav Stickley lamp table
with legs mortised through the flush circular top, arched cross-stretchers topped by a finial. Original finish on base, top refinished, good condition. 28 1/4" by 23 3/4"

$3,000-$3,500

Gustav Stickley lamp table
No. 436, with legs mortised through the top, and stacked cross stretchers topped by a finial. Excellent original finish, good condition, chew marks to finial. Early red decal. 28" by 23 1/2" diameter

$7,500-$8,500

Gustav Stickley lamp table
with flush circular top and arched cross-stretchers with finial. Refinished. Paper label. 29" by 30" diameter

$1,900-$2,300

L. & J.G. Stickley lamp table
with circular top and apron, and cross-stretchers mortised through the legs. Repair to apron, color added to top, base has original finish. Handcraft decal. 29" by 36" diameter

$900-$1,000

L.& J.G. Stickley lamp table
with circular overhanging top and apron over a lower shelf mortised through the posts. Refinished. Unmarked. 28 3/4" by 24" diameter

$1,400-$1,900

Tilt-top lamp table
attributed to J.M. Young (Camden, N.Y., 1890-1979), circa 1910-15, oak, original finish, 30" by 35" diameter

$900-$1,200

Tables, Library

Limbert library table
No. 134, rectangular top over blind drawers and lower shelf, single wide shaped slat on sides, refinished, paper label, overall roughness. 42" by 28" by 30"

$500-$600

Stickley Bros. library table
No. 2530, rectangular top over two half drawers with original brass hardware, through-tenon construction and Mackmurdo feet, worn original finish, stains and overall roughness. 48" by 28" by 30"

$650-$750

Tobey Furniture Co. library table
(Chicago, active 1857 to 1954) in mahogany, rectangular top over a single blind drawer and lower shelf, original finish, signed. 42" by 28" by 30"

$1,000-$1,500

Arts & Crafts library table
with blind drawer, slatted sides and lower shelf. Refinished. 27" by 30" by 24"

$300-$400

Limbert three-drawer library table

with overhanging top, hammered copper pulls and broad lower shelf. Good original finish. Branded mark. 29" by 60" by 32"

$2,000-$2,500

Limbert library table

with oval top, arched apron, and square cut-outs to flaring plank legs, with lower shelf. Refinished, separations to sides. Branded mark. 28 3/4" by 45" by 30"

$1,200-$1,700

Limbert single-drawer library table

with tacked-on Naugahyde top, three quarter-round corbels to either side, pyramidal copper pulls, and lower shelf. Original finish, missing some tacks. Branded mark. 29" by 42" by 26"

$800-$1,000

Limbert two-drawer library table

with a flush top and long corbels, square brass pulls. Refinished, good condition. Branded in drawer. 29" by 48" by 30 1/2"

$600-$800

Limbert two-drawer library table

with overhanging top, copper V-pulls, long corbels and broad lower shelf. Original finish, worn on top, seam separations and chips to legs. Branded mark. 29" by 48" by 34 1/4"

$1,000-$1,400

Limbert two-drawer library table

with square hammered copper pulls, arched apron and long corbels, with broad lower shelf tenoned through the stretcher. Refinished. Branded mark. 29" by 48" by 32"

$1,100-$1,500

Limbert oval library table

with cut-out flaring plank sides, arched aprons, corbels, and lower shelf. Some wear to original finish, good overall condition. Branded mark. 29" by 45" by 30"

$2,500-$3,200

Michigan Chair Co. single-drawer library table

with overhanging rectangular top, and lower shelf. Original finish with overcoat. Paper label. 30" by 48" by 30"

$600-$700

Shop of the Crafters clip-corner library table

(Cincinnati, Ohio, active 1904-20) with cut-out plank legs inlaid with ebonized and exotic woods, and cross-stretchers. Excellent original condition. Stenciled model number. 29" by 40" by 40 1/2"

$5,500-$6,500

Gustav Stickley library table

circa 1909-12, oak, original finish and iron hardware, replaced leather top and tacks, large black mark. 30" by 40" by 30"

$2,600-$2,900

Gustav Stickley library table

with single drawer and lower shelf. Refinished. Red decal. 30" by 48" by 29 1/2"

$1,500-$1,700

Gustav Stickley library table

with rectangular top and lower shelf keyed through the sides. Excellent original finish and condition. Paper label. 30" by 48" by 29 1/2"

$2,000-$2,500

Gustav Stickley library table

with two drawers, hammered copper pulls, long corbels, and lower shelf. Good original finish and condition. Paper label and partial red decal. 30" by 36" by 24"

$3,000-$3,500

Gustav Stickley two-drawer library table

with long corbels, broad cross stretcher and copper pulls. Overcoated original finish, bottom stretcher stripped of finish, minor chips and scuffs. Branded on side of drawer. 30" by 48" by 29 1/2"

$900-$1,100

Gustav Stickley two-drawer library table

with tacked-on new brown leather top, brass-washed hammered copper hardware, long corbels, and broad lower shelf. Original finish with color added and overcoat. Red decal inside drawer. 29" by 48" by 30"

$700-$1,000

Gustav Stickley two-drawer library table

with wrought iron hardware, long corbels, and broad lower shelf mortised through the stretchers. Refinished. Red decal. 30" by 54" by 31 1/2"

$1,800-$2,300

Gustav Stickley two-drawer library table

with overhanging rectangular top, hammered copper hardware, long corbels, and lower shelf mortised through side stretchers. Original finish to base, refinished top. Branded Stickley. 30" by 42" by 23 3/4"

$3,500-$4,000

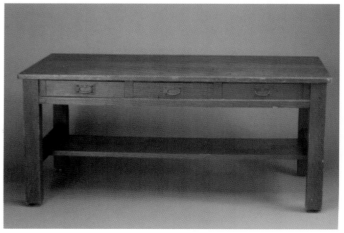

Gustav Stickley three-drawer library table

with oval pulls. Original finish, stains to top, a few scratches, and chips. Large red decal. 30 1/2" by 66" by 36"

$3,000-$4,000

Gustav Stickley three-drawer library table
with hammered copper pulls and long corbels. Restored finish to base, top is refinished. Large red decal under stretcher. 39" by 60" by 33 1/4"

$3,000-$3,750

Gustav Stickley three-drawer library table
with spindled sides, broad lower shelf, and hammered copper pulls. Original finish on base, top refinished, minor roughness to edges, small filled holes on left side. Red decal. 29" by 54" by 31"

$5,000-$6,000

Gustav Stickley three-drawer library table
with iron hardware and broad lower shelf. Original finish, seam separation and stains to top. Paper label and red decal. 29" by 66" by 36"

$4,500-$5,500

L. & J.G. Stickley library table
with arched apron and mortised stretcher. Dry original finish in need of restoration, overall very good condition. "The Work of..." decal. 29" by 48" by 30 1/4"

$1,500-$1,700

L. & J.G. Stickley library table
circa 1909-12, oak, original finish, shoe feet and trestle shelf, through tenons and keys. Handcraft mark. 29" by 48" by 30"

$3,500-$4,000

L. & J.G. Stickley library table
circa 1912-15, oak, original finish and hardware, through tenons and keys. 29" by 42" by 28"

$1,400-$1,600

L. & J.G. Stickley three-drawer library table
with overhanging top, long corbels, and mortised legs with broad lower shelf. Original finish to base, new finish to top, replaced hardware. Handcraft label. 29" by 60" by 32"

$3,500-$4,000

Stickley Bros. single-drawer library table
with overhanging rectangular top, two slats to each side, and lower shelf mortised through side stretchers. Good original finish. Quaint metal tag. 29" by 40" by 26"

$900-$1,100

Stickley Bros. two-drawer library table
with rectangular copper pulls, over double stretchers. Original finish, good condition, minor scratches to top. Quaint tag under stretcher. 30" by 66" by 38"

$2,000-$2,500

Stickley Bros. two-drawer library table
with overhanging rectangular top, copper drop pulls, slatted sides, double stretcher, on Mackmurdo-style feet. Original finish to base, refinished top. Unmarked. On casters (one broken): 29 1/2" by 46" by 29 3/4"

$750-$850

'Mackmurdo feet'

The design term "Mackmurdo feet"—which refers to an abruptly tapering or corseted leg with an angular flared foot—is in tribute to Arthur Heygate Mackmurdo (1851-1942), a disciple of John Ruskin and William Morris. In 1882, Mackmurdo founded the Century Guild in England, to produce work with Arts & Crafts designs.

Stickley Bros. two-drawer library table
with flush top, copper backplates and drop pulls, and lower shelf mortised through side stretchers, on Mackmurdo-style feet. Good original finish and condition. Stenciled number. 30" by 48" by 27 3/4"

$700-$900

Stickley Bros. two-drawer library table
No. 2442, with flush rectangular top, hammered copper drop pulls, and double plank stretcher mortised through the sides. Original finish, some looseness. Each drawer numbered 41. 30 1/4" by 54" by 32"

$1,750-$2,000

Stickley Bros. Quaint library table
circa 1912-1915, mahogany, refinished, original hardware, Mackmurdo feet. 29 1/2" by 42" by 28"

$800-$900

Tables, Library, Trestle

Rose Valley Association

The Rose Valley Association (1901-1909) in Rose Valley, Pa., was a utopian community near Philadelphia, making furniture and pottery.

Rose Valley trestle library table
with six butterfly joints in the top, carved trestle legs, and lower shelf keyed through the legs. Light overcoat to excellent original finish, drawer possibly added later, though appears to be period. Unmarked. 29" by 54" by 29 1/2"

$7,000-$9,000

Gustav Stickley trestle library table
with overhanging rectangular top, and lower shelf mortised with keyed through-tenons. Good original finish, separation and scratches in top, color loss around feet. Red decal. 29" by 48" by 29 3/4"

$1,700-$1,900

Gustav Stickley trestle library table

with rectangular top, and lower shelf double-keyed through the legs. Excellent original finish to base, skinned top, warped board, shaved edge. Red decal. 48" by 29" by 28"

$900-$1,250

L. & J.G. Stickley trestle library table

with double keyed through-tenon lower shelf. Original finish and condition, top scratched and stained. Handcraft label. 29" by 48" by 30"

$1,600-$1,800

L. & J.G. Stickley trestle library table

no. 596, with overhanging rectangular top and broad lower shelf keyed through the base. Good original finish and condition, minor staining to top. "The Work of..." metal tag. 29" by 66" by 24"

$4,000-$5,000

L. & J.G. Stickley trestle library table

with broad lower shelf mortised with two pairs of keyed through-tenons. Rough original finish and condition, with splits, color loss and separations. Red Handcraft decal. 29" by 48" by 30"

$1,200-$1,600

L.& J.G. Stickley trestle library table

with overhanging top, double-column sides and broad lower shelf keyed-through the sides. Original finish to base, cleaned finish with color added to top, seam separations to ends, dents and chipping around stretcher. Unmarked. 29" by 72" by 45"

$4,000-$5,000

Tables, Luncheon

Gustav Stickley lunch table
with original tacked-on leather top and medial stretcher fastened to side stretchers with keyed through-tenons. Fine original finish, wear and hole to leather, missing two tacks. Red decal. 29 1/2" by 40" by 30"
$4,200-$4,800

Gustav Stickley luncheon table
with overhanging rectangular top and keyed through-tenon stretcher. Excellent original finish to base, worn finish to top, some stains. Stickley box decal. 30" by 40" by 28"
$3,000-$4,000

Old Hickory luncheon table
with arched single-branch corbels. Original finish, break to one corbel. Branded mark. 30 1/2" by 36" square
$300-$400

Tables, Other

Arts & Crafts game table

circular wood top which can be flipped revealing a felt top and divided sections, single drawer over a cross stretcher base with through-tenon construction, some wear to original finish, needs gluing. 40" diameter by 30"

$550-$650

Arts & Crafts table

square top over lower shelf supported by stretchers with through-tenon details, original finish. 24" by 24" by 29"

$500-$700

Limbert table

in ash, rectangular top above a lower shelf with slab sides having two cutouts on a shoe-foot base, refinished, signed with early paper label. 36" by 24" by 30"

$1,500-$2,000

Limbert table

No. 101, octagonal top over four slab legs with cutouts and lower shelf, original finish, paper label. 31" by 31" by 29"

$1,200-$1,500

Limbert table

No. 146, oval top above lower shelf, slab sides with cutouts, original finish, branded. 45" by 30" by 29"

$2,300-$2,600

Limbert telephone table

No. 263, square top over an arched apron and lower shelf with tapered legs, lightly recoated original finish, branded. 18" by 18" by 29"

$400-$450

Michigan Chair Co. table

circular top over lower shelf with tapered legs, refinished, signed, with paper label. 18" diameter by 27"

$125-$175

Prairie School table

rectangular top over a lower shelf with molded trim and brass feet, original finish. 20" by 16" by 30"

$600-$700

Shop of the Crafters table

(Cincinnati, Ohio, active 1904-20) No. 110, cut corner rectangular top above a lower shelf supported by heavy slab sides with keyed tenon construction and cutout design, original finish, unsigned. 52" by 35" by 30"

$900-$1,200

Gustav Stickley table

No. 645, in mahogany, circular top and apron above an arched cross stretcher base, refinished, unsigned. 36" diameter by 29"

$1,500-$2,000

Gustav Stickley table

No. 648, circular top and apron over a notched lower stretcher with through-tenon construction and central finial, original finish to base, top refinished, signed with red decal. 36" diameter by 30"

$2,500-$3,000

L. & J.G. Stickley table

No. 954, form with rectangular top above a lower shelf and trestle base with double key and tenon construction, refinished, unsigned. 72" by 45" by 29"

$4,000-$4,500

Arts & Crafts tilt-top game table

that converts to a chair, with inlaid checkerboard top and diamond-shaped cutouts to legs. Very good original finish and condition. Unmarked. Dimensions as table: 28 3/4" by 25 1/2" square

$450-$650

Fine and rare tile-top sewing table

attributed to Catalina with a six-tile panel depicting birds of paradise in bright polychrome on black ground, mounted in a flip-top Mission table with turned legs. A few short scratches to tiles. Unmarked. Table: 24 1/4" by 27 1/4" by 17 1/4"

$3,500-$4,000

Gustav Stickley director's table

with overhanging rectangular top, broad apron, and shoe feet. Good original finish and color, (rarely found with original finish to top), screws holes under top. Red decal inside shoe foot. 30" by 72" by 36 1/2"

$25,000 to $30,000

Director's table

quaint style, circa 1912-15, oak, attributed to the Michigan Chair Co., Grand Rapids, shoe feet, original finish, 30" by 50" by 30"

$1,900-$2,200

L&JG Stickley round side table

circa 1915-20, oak, original finish, possibly made by J.M. Young, marked on bottom "125/540." 29" in. tall, 24" diameter

$1,800-$2,200

Lifetime circular table

with inset lower shelf on cross-stretchers. Refinished, reglued, some looseness. 29" by 24" diameter

$800-$1,000

Limbert pagoda table

with corbels under the square top, flaring sides with arched apron, lower shelf, and cutout base. Original finish, heavy overcoat. Paper label under top. 30 1/2" by 34" square

$10,000-$14,000

McHugh game table

(McHugh & Co., New York, active 1884 to 1916) with circular top, cross-banding to apron, keyed-through tenon ornamentation (two serving as drawer pulls, and two decorative) with arched cross-stretchers mortised through the legs. Original finish, crack to applied tenons. Partial paper label. 30 1/2" by 44 1/2" diameter

$1,500-$1,900

Charles Rohlfs octagonal table

with intricately cutout panels to the base, cabinet door with stamped hinges and latch, and two interior shelves. Overcoated original finish to base, top refinished, metal braces added under top. Unmarked. 28 3/4" by 32" diameter

$3,500-$4,500

Gustav Stickley stacked-stretcher drum-top table

1903, oak, original finish, large red mark, near mint. 30" by 40" diameter

$7,000-$8,000

Gustav Stickley table
with circular top, keyhole four-sided apron, and turned flaring legs. Good original finish.
Unmarked. 24 1/2" by 24" diameter

$1,250-$1,750

L. & J.G. Stickley clip-corner table
with lower shelf on arched cross-stretcher. Original finish to base, top refinished.
Branded mark. 29 1/2" by 18" square

$700-$900

L. & J.G. Stickley clip-corner side table
with square lower shelf supported by arched cross-stretchers. Very good original finish
and condition. "The Work of..." decal. 29 1/4" by 18" square

$900-$1,400

L. & J.G. Stickley encyclopedia book table
with square top and four cubbies with slatted sides. Base has original finish, top is
refinished, small spot of deep scratches and staining to top, chipping to legs of base.
Handcraft label. 29" by 27" square

$7,000-$8,000

Tables, Serving

Stickley Bros. serving table
No. 2900, removable glass tray with copper handles on a rectangular table with flared legs and a central caned panel, original finish, unsigned. 25" by 17" by 29"

$1,200-$1,500

Stickley Bros. single-drawer table
with flush top, three slats to each side, and lower shelf. Some wear to original finish, stain and seam separation to top. Unmarked. 30" by 24" by 22"

$2,500-$3,000

Lifetime Puritan Line single-drawer serving table
with arched apron and low stretchers. Original finish, good condition, veneer chip to right side. Paper label. 36" by 40" by 18 1/2"

$1,200-$1,600

Tables, Side

Arts & Crafts round side table
circa 1915-20, oak, original finish, possibly made by J.M. Young (Camden, N.Y., 1890 to 1979), marked on bottom "125/540." 29" tall, 24" diameter

$1,800-$2,200

Gustav Stickley side table
circa 1901, oak, original finish, arched crossed stretchers, through tenons and keys, slab legs, arched apron and clip-corner top, rare form, unmarked. 29" by 36" by 28"

$35,000-$45,000

Stickley Bros. side table
with pyramidal posts, a single drawer and lower shelf, and a hall chair with three vertical back slats and cutout top. Both have overcoated original finish, replaced knobs on side table. Chair has Quaint tag. 29" by 21" by 16 1/2", and 37 1/2" by 16" by 15 1/2"
$1,000-$1,250/pair

Stickley Bros. side table
with copper-clad circular top and X-shaped stretcher mortised through flaring legs. Original finish with overcoat, some roughness. Stenciled 406-2864. 26" by 25"
$2,000-$2,500

Tables, Tea

Limbert circular tea table
with arched stretchers mortised through tapering posts. New finish, small scratch to top. Branded. 29" by 42" diameter
$1,100-$1,400

Gustav Stickley tea table
with circular top over cross stretchers. Refinished, good condition. Branded mark. 29" by 23 1/2" diameter
$1,000-$1,400

L. & J.G. Stickley circular tea table
with lower shelf. Original finish with overcoat, some looseness. Branded. 24" by 20" diameter

$2,000-$2,500

Stickley Bros. tea table
with overhanging square top and clip-corner lower shelf over cross-stretchers, on tapering legs. Original finish, very good condition. Unmarked. 29 1/2" by 24" square

$950-$1,250

Stickley Bros. teacart
with tray top set with original glass, turned posts, and lower shelf. Original finish, repair to center of one wheel, missing rubber tires. Branded mark. 29 1/2" by 28" by 18"

$450-$550

Tables, Trestle

Gustav Stickley trestle table
No. 637, original finish, original leather and tacks, signed with paper label. 48" by 30" by 28 1/2"

$4,000-$5,000

Arts & Crafts trestle-leg dining table
with keyed-through stretcher. Refinished, some looseness. Unmarked. 29 1/2" by 90" by 32"

$1,200-$1,500

Charles Stickley trestle table
with broad lower shelf keyed through double planks. Good original finish and condition with some staining to top. Unmarked. 28 1/2" by 48" by 30"

$700-$900

Charles Stickley trestle table
with overhanging top and lower shelf with keyed through tenons. Original finish, good condition. Stickley-Brandt label inside leg. 29" by 48" by 30"

$700-$900

L. & J.G. Stickley mouse-hole trestle table
No. 599, with rectangular top and keyed broad stretcher. Good original finish to base, cleaned original finish to top, with stain. Unmarked. 29" by 48" by 32"

$1,800-$2,200

Taborets

The word taboret dates to the early 17th century. It is French in origin and means "small drum." The term is usually applied to a small portable stand or cabinet, or a cylindrical seat or stool without arms or back. It is sometimes spelled "tabouret."

Arts & Crafts taboret
in the style of Limbert, hexagonal top over three-leg base with spade cutouts, cleaned original finish. 11" by 18"

$200-$300

Arts & Crafts taboret
similar to Gustav Stickley No. 601, circular top with arched lower stretcher, probably not old, refinished. 14" by 16"

$125-$175

Arts & Crafts taboret
square top over flared base with corbel supports and oval cutouts, refinished. 15" by 15" by 18"

$450-$550

Arts & Crafts taboret
circular top over three-leg base with organic cutouts, refinished. 16" by 17"

$100-$150

Arts & Crafts taboret
three-sided form with clip-corner top over splayed legs with lower shelf, refinished. 15" by 17" by 20"

$175-$225

Limbert taboret
No. 211, square top over flared legs, original finish, branded signature. 12" square by 16"

$300-$400

Gustav Stickley taboret
square top above four legs, original finish, branded signature. 14" by 14" by 20"

$400-$500

L. & J.G. Stickley taboret
No. 559, octagonal top with through-post construction over arched cross stretchers, original finish, signed "The work of..." minor factory flaw at edge. 18" by 18" by 20"

$800-$900

L. & J.G. Stickley taboret
No. 561, clip-corner square top over a single wide slat and arched lower stretchers on each side, refinished, unsigned. 20" by 20" by 22"

$1,100-$1,400

Arts & Crafts taboret
with hexagonal brass-clad top, "cloud-lift" stretchers, and six flaring legs. Refinished. Unmarked. 24" by 18 3/4"

$1,100-$1,400

'Cloud-lift'

The term "cloud-lift" refers to the modification of a traditional arched stretcher or apron by giving the bottom edges a straight—rather than curving—profile at the ends. This design motif can often be seen in early Chinese furniture forms.

Limbert taboret
with square top and box construction with square cutouts. Original finish on base, top refinished. Branded mark. 18" by 16 1/2" square

$2,000-$2,500

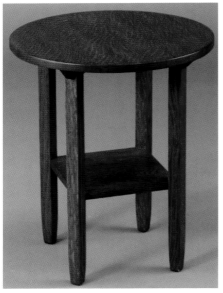

Limbert taboret

with circular top, tapered posts, and square lower shelf. Good new finish. Branded mark. 22" by 18 1/2" diameter

$850-$1,000

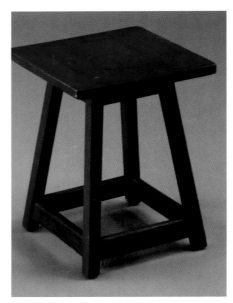

Limbert taboret

with square top, and flaring legs joined by stretchers. Overcoated top, original finish to base. Branded mark. 16" by 12" square

$1,000-$1,400

Gustav Stickley circular taboret

with "cloud-lift" cross stretchers. Breaks to one stretcher and reglued leg, refinished. Branded mark. 16" by 14"

$300-$400

Gustav Stickley Lotus mahogany taboret

with pentagonal top, five cutout legs and star-shaped stretcher below. Overcoated original finish. Remnant of early paper label. 20" by 19"

$2,200-$2,600

Gustav Stickley taboret

with circular top and "cloud-lift" cross stretchers. Refinished top, good original finish to base, good condition. 18" by 16" diameter

$800-$1,000

Gustav Stickley taboret

with circular top and "cloud-lift" cross-stretchers. Refinished. Unmarked. 17 3/4" by 16" diameter

$1,200-$1,500

L. & J.G. Stickley clip-corner taboret
with overhanging top and arched through-tenon cross stretchers. Original finish, good condition. Handcraft decal. 18" by 16"

$450-$550

L. & J.G. Stickley octagonal taboret
No. 558, with cross-stretchers. Overcoated original finish. Branded mark. 17" by 15" diameter

$700-$800

L. & J.G. Stickley octagonal taboret
No. 559, with cross stretchers. Restored finish to base, top refinished. Handcraft decal. 20 1/4" by 18" diameter

$1,100-$1,300

L. & J.G. Stickley octagonal taboret
with its legs mortised through the top, and cross-stretchers. Original finish, wear to top, good condition. "The Work of..." label. 17" by 15"

$800-$1,000

L. & J.G. Stickley octagonal taboret
with legs mortised through the top, above cross-stretchers. Original finish, good condition. Unsigned. 20 1/4" by 18" diameter

$900-$1,200

L. & J.G. Stickley taboret
with arched stretchers. Good condition, refinished. Unmarked. 20" by 18" square

$950-$1,250

Taboret
attributed to L. & J.G. Stickley, No. 781, with circular overhanging top and bracketed cross stretchers. Original finish, very good condition. 18" by 16" diameter

$500-$700

Stickley Bros. square taboret
with two level stretchers. Original finish, minor staining to top, excellent condition. Unmarked. 16 1/4" by 13"

$500-$600

Stickley Bros. taboret
No. 138, with square posts through the top, Mackmurdo feet. Refinished. Unmarked. 18" by 13 3/4" square

$500-$600

'Mackmurdo feet'

The design term "Mackmurdo feet" — which refers to an abruptly tapering or corseted leg with an angular flared foot — is in tribute to Arthur Heygate Mackmurdo (1851-1942), a disciple of John Ruskin and William Morris. In 1882, Mackmurdo founded the Century Guild in England, to produce work with Arts & Crafts designs.

Stickley Bros. taboret
circa 1908, oak, refinished, with cutout legs, indistinct mark. 18 1/2" tall, 17 1/2" wide

$700-$900

Umbrella Stands

Arts & Crafts umbrella holder
probably English, four-sided form with deeply carved
flower and leaf design, original drip pan, original finish.
12" by 12" by 20"

$200-$250

**Roycroft
hexagonal
umbrella stand**
designed by William
Roth, 1910, with three
cutout sides with riveted
hammered copper straps
and original drip pan.
Fine original finish.
Unmarked. 30" by 12"
$1,900-$2,300

Vanities

Limbert single-drawer vanity
with pivoting mirror, copper hardware, and H-shaped stretcher mortised through the legs. Original finish, good condition. Branded mark. 58 1/2" by 36" by 24 1/2"
$1,500-$2,000

Gustav Stickley five-drawer vanity
No. 907, with integrated mirror and wrought-iron ring pulls. Some wear to original finish, seam separations, sagging to drawer bank, reglued. Red decal in center drawer. 55" by 48" by 22"
$3,300-$4,000

Gustav Stickley two-drawer vanity
No. 914, with overhanging top, arched apron and wooden mushroom pulls. Original finish, good condition. Red decal in right drawer. 54" by 36" by 18 1/2"
$2,000-$2,500

Gustav Stickley vanity
designed by Harvey Ellis, with two drawers with circular wooden pulls, arched apron, tapering posts and attached pivot mirror with two butterfly joints. Original finish to base and mirror, refinished top. Red decal. 53" by 36" by 17 3/4"
$2,700-$3,300

Gustav Stickley five-drawer vanity
with cast oval pulls, and pivoting mirror flanked by copper candlesconces (one bobeche missing). Original finish, seam separation and stains to top, missing lock. 1902 decal. 57 1/4" by 54" by 22 1/4"
$6,000-$7,000

Wardrobe
(Also see Armoires)

Gustav Stickley wardrobe
with two paneled doors enclosing an interior with five half-drawers over a full one, hammered copper V-pulls, and arched toe board. Good condition, overcoated original finish, repaired holes on both sides. Paper label and red decal. 62" by 43" by 24"
$8,000-$10,000

Washstand

Gustav Stickley washstand
with vertical slatted backsplash, two drawers with iron pulls, and lower shelf. Good original finish and condition, minor stains to top. Unmarked. 45" by 40" by 20"
$7,000-$9,000

Wastebaskets

Arts & Crafts wastebasket
notched slatted sides above an arched lower support, cleaned original finish. 13" by 13" by 20"
$400-$450

Hexagonal wastebasket
attributed to Charles Rohlfs, with wedged posts and tulip cut-out to panels. Original finish, small sliver missing from upright, otherwise excellent condition. Unmarked. 17" by 14"

$2,000-$2,500

Gustav Stickley slatted wastebasket
the slats riveted to interior iron hoops. Original finish, good condition. Red decal and partial paper label. 14" by 12"

$2,800-$3,200

Gustav Stickley slatted wastebasket
the slats riveted to interior iron hoops. Original finish, minor wear. Paper label on bottom. 14" by 12"

$1,250-$1,600

Stickley Bros. flared wastebasket
with two cutout handles and five slats to each side. Good original finish and condition. Stenciled 80, with Quaint metal tag. 17 1/2" by 14 1/4"

$950-$1,250

Ads

The next several pages featuring Arts & Crafts furniture are taken from an early 20th century catalog issued by Janney, Semple, Hill & Co. of Minneapolis. "We have endeavored to print under one cover the best and most popular merchandise of leading manufacturers of their respective lines," the catalog says. "Our attractive prices and modern facilities for prompt shipment should receive your most careful attention."

No. 545C397— 6-ft.—EXTENSION TABLE.............. $20.00
No. 545C397— 8-ft.—EXTENSION TABLE.............. 25.00
No. 545C397—10-ft.—EXTENSION TABLE.............. 29.00

Made of oak with 45-in. plain oak top. Finished G. O. polished and fumed. Has non-dividing pedestal. In 8 and 10-ft. lengths the top has drop leg supports which fold under when top is closed. Weight in 6-ft., about 180 pounds.

No. 545Q397— 6-ft.—EXTENSION TABLE.............. $24.00
No. 545Q397— 8-ft.—EXTENSION TABLE.............. 30.00
No. 545Q397—10-ft.—EXTENSION TABLE.............. 33.00

Same as above with quartered oak top.

No. 542C395— 6-ft.—EXTENSION TABLE.............. $15.00
No. 542C395— 8-ft.—EXTENSION TABLE.............. 20.00
No. 542C395—10-ft.—EXTENSION TABLE.............. 23.00

Made of oak with 42-in. plain oak top. Finished in G. O. and fumed. Has non-dividing pedestal. In 8 and 10-ft. lengths top is equipped with drop leg supports which fold under when top is closed. Weight in 6-ft., about 140 pounds.

	42-in. Top.	45-in. Top
No. 45590— 6-ft.—EXTENSION TABLE......	$17.00	$18.95
No. 45590— 8-ft.—EXTENSION TABLE......	22.00	23.95
No. 44490—10-ft.—EXTENSION TABLE......	24.75	27.90

Imitation quartered oak; polished top; 8-in. pedestal; non-dividing. Four drop legs to support 8-ft. and 10-ft. tables when extended. Also made in 12-ft. Castered.

Shipping weight about 120 pounds.

Janney, Semple, Hill & Co. Minneapolis.

112

No. 5220—LIBRARY TABLE $31.00

Made of quarter sawed oak. 28x48 top in plank effect. Finished in golden flat or fumed. K. D. construction. Weight, about 155 pounds.

No. 5222—LIBRARY TABLE $30.00

Quartered oak with 28x48 top in plank effect. Finished in golden oak or fumed. Two drawers in top. K. D. construction. Weight, about 155 pounds.

Janney, Semple, Hill & Co. Minneapolis.

113

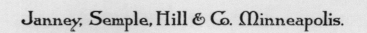

No. 5186—LIBRARY TABLE $31.00

Made of selected quarter sawed white oak. Finished in G. O. waxed, Early English and fumed. Top, 28x48. Shipped S. U. Weight, 140 pounds.

No. 5205—LIBRARY TABLE $33.00

Made of selected quarter sawed oak. Top, 28x48. Finished G. O. waxed and fumed. Has cane panels in ends. K. D. construction. Weight, 125 pounds.

114 **Janney, Semple, Hill & Co. Minneapolis.**

No. 5219—LIBRARY TABLE............................ $24.00

Made of quarter sawed oak. 28x48 top in plank effect. Finished golden oak or fumed. K. D. construction. Weight, about 135 pounds.

No. 5217—LIBRARY TABLE............................ $28.00

Made of quarter sawed oak. Top, 28x48, in plank effect. Finished golden oak or fumed. K. D. construction. Weight, about 140 pounds.

Janney, Semple, Hill & Co. Minneapolis. 117

No. 5218—LIBRARY TABLE............................ $20.00

Made of oak with quartered oak top, 26x42, in plank effect. Finished golden oak or fumed. Drawer in top. K. D. construction. Weight, about 110 pounds.

No. 5201—LIBRARY TABLE............................ $21.00

Made of quarter sawed oak. Top, 26x42. Finished G. O. waxed and fumed. Shipped S. U. Weight, about 110 pounds.

Janney, Semple, Hill & Co. Minneapolis.

No. 5208—LIBRARY TABLE.............................$16.00

Made of quarter sawed oak. Finished G. O., waxed and fumed. Top, 26x42. K. D. construction. Weight, about 85 pounds.

No. 5204—LIBRARY TABLE.............................$14.00

Made of quarter sawed oak. Finished G. O., waxed and fumed. Top, 24x40. K. D. construction. Weight, about 80 pounds.

Janney, Semple, Hill & Co. Minneapolis.

No. 44810—LIBRARY TABLE.............................$11.00

Imitation quartered oak. Golden polish or fumed finish on birch. Plank edge top, 26x42. Drawer. 3-in. legs. Weight, 90 pounds.

No. 45000—LIBRARY TABLE.............................$10.00

Imitation quartered oak on birch. Polished top, 24x36. 2½-in. legs. Weight, 70 pounds.

124 Janney, Semple, Hill & Co. Minneapolis.

No. 44480—BED ROOM TABLE............................ $6.60
Imitation quartered oak. Golden or fumed finish on birch.
Top, 20x28. Weight, 40 pounds.

No. 44470—BED ROOM TABLE............................ $5.00
Imitation quartered oak. Golden or fumed finish on birch.
Top, 18x24. Weight, 35 pounds.

Janney, Semple, Hill & Co. Minneapolis. 127

5C42

5C40

5C51

5C52

No. 5C42—TELEPHONE SET, Price.......... $15.00
Golden wax or fumed oak. Table, 15x22, 29
inches high. Chair seat, 18 inches high.

No. 5C40—TELEPHONE SET, Price.......... $11.50
Golden wax or fumed oak. Table, 17x17; 29
inches high. Stool, 18 inches high with groove slide
to fit under table.

No. 5C51—SMOKING TABLE, Price.......... $6.60
Golden wax or fumed oak. Top, 14x14. Height,
28 inches.

No. 5C52—SMOKING TABLE, Price.......... $5.50
Golden wax or fumed oak. Top, 12x12. Height,
28 inches.

No. 530—PEDESTAL........ $5.50
Oak. Finished G. O. and fumed.
Top, 12 in. Height, 36 in. Weight,
36 pounds.

No. 537—PEDESTAL........ $6.50
Imitation quartered oak on birch.
Finished golden. Height, 36 in.
Top, 13 in. Weight, 45 pounds.

No. 536—PEDESTAL........ $3.80
Imitation quartered oak on birch.
Finished golden. Height, 36 in.
Top, 12x12. Weight, 35 pounds.

No. 5630—DESK........................ $27.00
Made of quartered oak. Finished G. O.
flat or fumed. Height, 40 in. Width, 33 in.
Weight, about 120 pounds.

No. 5627—DESK........................ $20.00
Made of quarter sawed oak. Finished G.
O. waxed and fumed. Height, 43 in. Width,
32 in. Weight, about 75 pounds.

No. 5605—DESK........................ $19.00

Quartered oak. Fumed, Early English or
golden polish finish. Height, 43 in. Width,
33 in. Weight, 100 pounds.

No. 5108—ROLL TOP DESK........................... $22.00

Plain oak. Finished light golden gloss. Dust proof curtain.
Length, 42 in. Depth, 30 in. Height, 45 in. Weight, 140 pounds.
Shipped K. D.

Janney, Semple, Hill & Co. Minneapolis. 143

No. 5561—SECTIONAL CASE...................... $38.50

Quartered oak. Finished G. O. or fumed. Six-unit case consisting of top and bottom sections and four book sections, corresponding in dimensions and grouping to the units of No. 5559L, section case described elsewhere.

No. 5560—SECTIONAL CASE........................ $36.00

Quartered oak. Finished G. O. or fumed. A six-unit case consisting of top and bottom sections with four book sections corresponding in dimensions and grouping to the grouping of No. 5559L sectional case described elsewhere.

Janney, Semple, Hill & Co. Minneapolis. 155

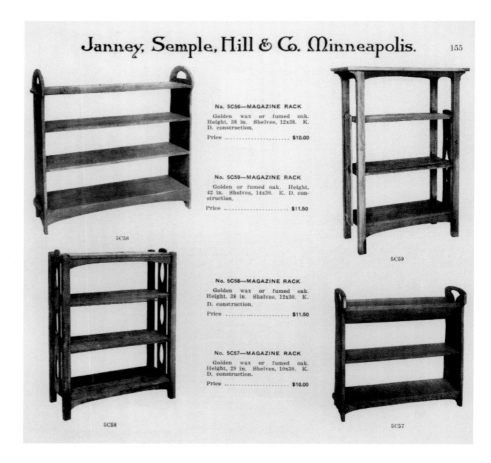

No. 5C56—MAGAZINE RACK

Golden wax or fumed oak. Height, 38 in. Shelves, 12x38. K. D. construction.

Price $10.00

No. 5C59—MAGAZINE RACK

Golden or fumed oak. Height, 42 in. Shelves, 14x36. K. D. construction.

Price $11.50

No. 5C58—MAGAZINE RACK

Golden wax or fumed oak. Height, 38 in. Shelves, 12x30. K. D. construction.

Price $11.50

No. 5C57—MAGAZINE RACK

Golden wax or fumed oak. Height, 29 in. Shelves, 10x30. K. D. construction.

Price $10.00

5C56

5C59

5C58

5C57

No. 5C55—MAGAZINE RACK
Golden wax or fumed oak.
Height, 36 in. Shelves, 12x16.
K. D. construction.
Price $5.00

No. 5C53—MAGAZINE RACK
Golden wax or fumed oak.
Height, 45 in. Shelves 13x18.
K. D. construction.
Price $7.00

No. 5C47—UMBRELLA RACK
Golden wax or fumed oak.
Base, 10x17. Height, 50 in.
Large shelf at top. Heavy
brass drain plate.
Price $9.50

No. 5C44—UMBRELLA RACK
Golden wax or fumed oak.
Base, 12x12. Height, 28 in.
Heavy brass drain plate.
Price $6.60

No. 5C45—UMBRELLA RACK
Golden wax or fumed oak.
Base, 12x15. Height, 36 in.
Heavy brass drain plate.
Price $6.60

No. 5C46—UMBRELLA RACK
Golden wax or fumed oak.
Base, 12x12. Height, 24 in.
Heavy brass drain plate.
Price $3.80

No. 5C43—UMBRELLA RACK
Golden wax or fumed oak.
Base, 12x12. Height, 28 in.
Heavy brass drain plate.
Price $5.50

5C55 5C53 5C47 5C44 5C45 5C46 5C43

Janney, Semple, Hill & Co. Minneapolis.

157

No. 560—MAGAZINE RACK $5.50
Made of oak. Fumed finish only. Height, 39 in. Width, 18
in. Depth, 13 in. Weight, about 25 pounds. Shipped K. D.

No. 561—MAGAZINE RACK $5.50
Made of oak. Fumed finish only. Height, 30 in. Width, 32
in. Depth, 13 in. Weight, about 25 pounds. Shipped K. D.

No. 570—STUDENT'S STAND $4.00
Ash, golden finish. Top, 20x36. No drawer.

No. 571—STUDENT'S STAND $4.50
Same as above, with drawer.

No. 573—STUDENT TABLE $9.00
Quartered oak. Finished G. O., Early English and fumed.
Top, 18x28. With drawer. K. D. construction. Weight, 35
pounds.

No. 572—STUDENT TABLE $8.50
Same as above with no drawer.

Janney, Semple, Hill & Co. Minneapolis.

173

No. 21323 MISSION SUIT—THREE PIECES.

Sofa, length, 50 in.; height, 44 in. Made of selected quartersawed oak. Finished in golden or fumed oak. Hand rubbed. Solid board bottom, which makes it everlasting. Cushions are filled with pure white cotton. Edges of cushions sewed, not laced, as shown.

	Boston Leather	Mole Skin	No. 1 Leather
Sofa	$46.70	$50.60	$69.30
Rocker	27.50	30.80	39.60
Easy	26.40	29.70	38.50
Full suit	$100.10	$111.10	$147.40

IMPORTANT—Be sure to specify finish of Woodwork desired, also whether Black or Brown Spanish Leather. No. 1 Leather is always furnished unless otherwise ordered.

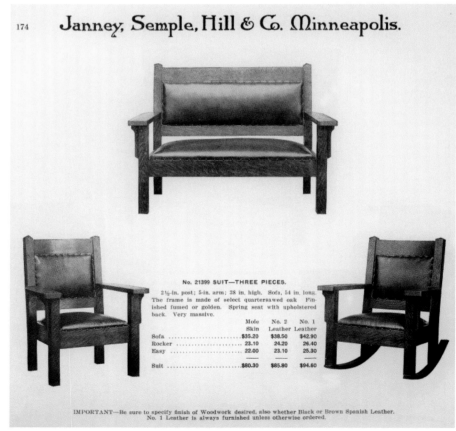

174

Janney, Semple, Hill & Co. Minneapolis.

No. 21399 SUIT—THREE PIECES.

2½-in. post; 5-in. arm; 38 in. high. Sofa, 54 in. long. The frame is made of select quartersawed oak. Finished fumed or golden. Spring seat with upholstered back. Very massive.

	Mole Skin	No. 2 Leather	No. 1 Leather
Sofa	$35.20	$38.50	$42.90
Rocker	23.10	24.20	26.40
Easy	22.00	23.10	25.30
Suit	$80.30	$85.80	$94.60

IMPORTANT—Be sure to specify finish of Woodwork desired, also whether Black or Brown Spanish Leather. No. 1 Leather is always furnished unless otherwise ordered.

Janney, Semple, Hill & Co. Minneapolis.

No. 21300 MISSION SUIT—THREE PIECES.

Sofa, 48 in. long. Suit stands 38 in. high. Made of quartersawed oak. Finished in golden or fumed oak. Hand rubbed. Full spring seats and upholstered backs.

	Boston	Mole Skin	No. 2 Leather	No. 1 Leather
Sofa	$24.20	$26.40	$29.20	$34.10
Rocker	16.00	17.00	17.60	19.80
Easy	14.90	16.00	16.50	18.70
Suit	$55.10	$59.40	$63.30	$72.60

IMPORTANT—Be sure to specify finish of Woodwork desired, also whether Black or Brown Spanish Leather. No. 1 Leather is always furnished unless otherwise ordered.

Closed.

No. 202073—DUOFOLD BED

Selected quartersawed oak or birch. Mahogany finish. 4-in. arm, 36 in. high, 61 in. long, outside measurement.

Boston leather, black or Spanish	$42.90
Mole skin, black or Spanish	47.30
No. 2 leather, black or Spanish	55.00
No. 1 guaranteed leather, black or Spanish	66.00

No. 202041—DUOFOLD BED

Select quartersawed oak, any finish. 3½-in. arm; 36 in. high, 60 in. long, outside measurement.

Boston leather, black or Spanish	$58.30
Mole skin, black or Spanish	62.00
No. 2 leather, black or Spanish	66.00
No. 1 guaranteed leather, black or Spanish	77.00

IMPORTANT—Be sure to specify finish of Woodwork desired, also whether Black or Brown Spanish Leather. No. 1 Leather is always furnished unless otherwise ordered.

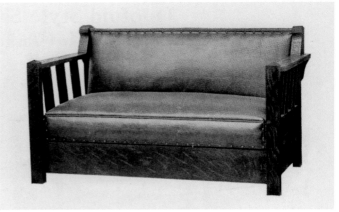

No. 202048—DUOFOLD BED

Select quartersawed oak, any finish. 5 in. arm; 5 in. post; 35 in. high; 63 in. long, outside measure.

Boston leather, black or Spanish........................ $66.00
Mole skin, black or Spanish............................ 70.00
No. 2 leather, black or Spanish........................ 77.00
No. 1 guaranteed leather, black or Spanish.............. 86.00
"K." Tapestry.. 79.00

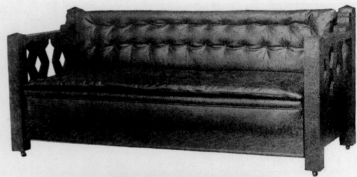

No. 22051—PULLMAN DAVENPORT

Saddle seat and back. Quartersawed oak, any finish. 3½ in. post. 3½x2 in. arm. 81 in. long. The saddle seat is used to give it special comfort while used as a davenport. The cushions are filled with best white cotton.

Boston leather, black or Spanish........................ $84.00
Mole skin, black or Spanish............................ 92.40
No. 2 leather, black or Spanish........................ 101.20
No. 1 leather (guaranteed) black or Spanish............ 120.00

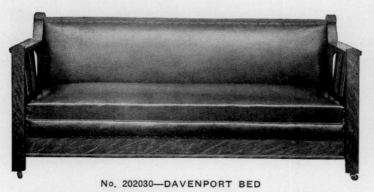

No. 202030—DAVENPORT BED

Selected quartersawed oak, any finish. 3 in. post; 37 in. high; 31 in. wide; 81 in. long, outside measurement.

Boston leather, black or Spanish........................ $55.00
Mole skin, black or Spanish............................ 59.00
No. 2 leather, black or Spanish........................ 68.00
No. 1 guaranteed leather, black or Spanish.............. 84.00

No. 202065—DAVENPORT BED

Select quartersawed oak, any finish. 3¼ in. post; 37½ in. high; 31x81 in., outside measurement.

Boston leather, black or Spanish	$59.00
Mole skin, black or Spanish	63.00
No. 2 leather, black or Spanish	70.00
No. 1 guaranteed leather, black or Spanish	86.00

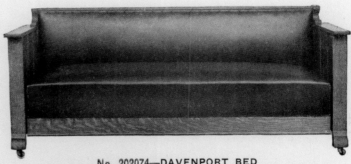

No. 202074—DAVENPORT BED

Birch, mahogany finish, or quartersawed oak, any finish. 4 in. arm; 36 in. high; 82 in. long, outside measurement.

Mole Skin, black or Spanish	$51.00
Boston leather, black or Spanish	46.00
No. 2 leather, black or Spanish	62.00
No. 1 guaranteed leather, black or Spanish	72.00
Tapestry	64.00

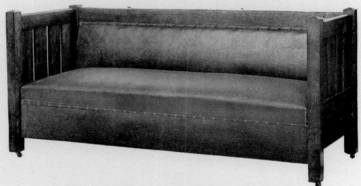

No. 202075—DAVENPORT BED

Select quartersawed oak, any finish. 2½ in. arm; 2½ in. post; 38 in. high; 79 in. long, outside measurements.

Boston leather, black or Spanish	$57.00
Mole skin, black or Spanish	62.00
No. 2 leather, black or Spanish	68.00
No. 1 guaranteed leather, black or Spanish	83.00

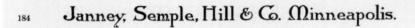

Janney, Semple, Hill & Co. Minneapolis.

184

No. 2300—SADDLE SEAT AND HEAD COUCH

26 in. wide, 74 in. long. Spring edge, a new feature for comfort. Cushions are attached and filled with pure white Southern cotton. Finished in fumed or golden oak.

Boston leather, black or Spanish....	$44.00
Mole skin, black or Spanish........	50.00
No. 2 leather (not guaranteed) black or Spanish.................	66.00
No. 1 leather (guaranteed) black or Spanish	86.00
"K." Tapestry......................	70.00

No. 3981—MISSION COUCH

Selected quartersawed oak frame; extra heavy. Best steel spring construction used. Hair filling. Fumed or golden oak finish. Upholstered in No. 1 black or Spanish leather $66.00

IMPORTANT—Be sure to specify finish of Woodwork desired, also whether Black or Brown Spanish Leather.

No. 21083—MISSION FOOT REST

Oak; golden, weathered or early English.
Size, 8x16x15 in. high.

Black or Spanish leather................................. $4.50

No. 21492—MISSION FOOT REST

Oak. Golden, weathered or early English. Size, 10x18x15 in. high.
Leather $5.50

No. 3364—MISSION ROCKER

Fitted with spring cushion back and seat. Height 40 in., width 31 in., depth 26 in. Arm chair to match. This rocker is a wonder for comfort, and biggest seller we have had on our floor. Finished golden oak and fumed oak.

No. 1 goat skin	$43.00
No. 1 Spanish or black leather	46.00
Mole skin	35.00
"C." Tapestry	38.00

No. 3316—MISSION ROCKER

Fitted with cushion spring seat and upholstered back. Height 40 in., width 28 in. Arm chair to match. Finished golden oak or fumed oak.

No. 1 goat skin	$36.00
No. 1 Spanish or black leather	38.00
Mole skin	29.00
"C." Tapestry	31.00

IMPORTANT—Be sure to specify finish of Woodwork desired, also whether Black or Brown Spanish Leather. No. 1 Leather is always furnished unless otherwise ordered.

No. 21589½—EASY ROCKER

Quartersawed oak. Polished or dull. Fumed or golden finish. Very large and comfortable. 40 in. high.

Boston leather, black or Spanish	$28.50
Mole skin, black or Spanish	31.00
No. 2 leather, black or Spanish	34.00
No. 1 guaranteed leather, black or Spanish	38.00

No. 3363—QUARTERED OAK

Finished golden or fumed. Highly polished or dull. Full spring seat. Height, 42 in.; width, 29 in.; depth, 20 in.

No. 1 black leather	$27.50
Spanish leather	27.50
Mole skin	25.00

Janney, Semple, Hill & Co. Minneapolis.

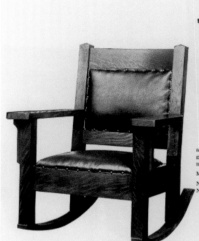

No. 21684½—ROCKER

Quartersawed oak. 2-in. post; 4-in. arm; 38 in. high. Finished fumed or golden oak. Pad back with a loose automobile cushion seat.

Mole skin, black or Spanish...... $19.00
No. 2 leather, black or Spanish.... 20.50
No. 1 guaranteed leather, black or
Spanish 24.00

No. 21670½—MISSION ROCKER

Quartersawed oak, finished fumed or golden oak. 2½-in. posts; 5-in. arms; 36 in. high.

Mole skin, black or Spanish.................. $23.00
No. 2 leather, black or Spanish.............. 24.00
No. 1 guaranteed leather, black or Spanish... 27.00
Arm chair to match.

No. 21671½—AUTO SEAT ROCKER

Quartersawed oak. Finished fumed or golden oak. 2½-in. posts; 5-in. arms; 37 in. high. Upholstered back with loose automobile cushion seat.

Mole skin, black or Spanish.................. $25.00
No. 2 leather, black or Spanish.............. 27.50
No. 1 guaranteed leather, black or Spanish.. 31.00

IMPORTANT—Be sure to specify finish of Woodwork desired, also whether Black or Brown Spanish Leather.
No. 1 Leather is always furnished unless otherwise ordered.

Janney, Semple, Hill & Co. Minneapolis.

203

No. 21692½—MISSION ROCKER

Select quartersawed oak, any finish. 2½-in. post; 4-in. arm; 34 in. high.

Mole skin, black or Spanish...... $24.00
No. 2 leather, black or Spanish.... 25.00
No. 1 leather, black or Spanish.... 29.00

Arm Chair to Match, Same Price.

No. 21681½—AUTO SEAT ROCKER

Quartersawed oak. 2½-in. post; 4¾-in. arm; 37½ in. high. Finished in fumed oak or golden oak. Upholstered back and automobile cushion seat.

Mole skin, black or Spanish.................. $20.00
No. 2 leather, black or Spanish.............. 22.00
No. 1 guaranteed leather, black or Spanish..... 25.00

No. 21679½—AUTO SEAT ROCKER

Quartersawed oak. 2-in. post; 4 in. arm; 38 in. high. Finished fumed or golden oak. Pad back with a loose automobile cushion seat.

Mole skin, black or Spanish.................. $15.50
No. 2 leather, black or Spanish.............. 19.00
No. 1 guaranteed leather, black or Spanish... 22.00

IMPORTANT—Be sure to specify finish of Woodwork desired, also whether Black or Brown Spanish Leather.
No. 1 Leather is always furnished unless otherwise ordered.

Janney, Semple, Hill & Co. Minneapolis.

No. 3282—MISSION ROCKER

Fitted with loose automobile seat and upholstered back. Height, 38 in.; width, 30 in.; depth, 20 in. Finished golden and fumed.

No. 1 Spanish or black leather....	$20.00
Mole skin.........................	17.00

No. 3287—MISSION ROCKER

Fitted with loose spring seat cushion. Height, 35 in.; width, 28 in.; depth, 19 in. Finished golden or fumed.

No. 1 black leather.......................	$13.00
Spanish leather...........................	13.00
Mole skin.................................	12.00

No. 3374—MISSION ROCKER

Fitted with spring seat. Height, 35 in.; width, 29 in.; depth, 20 in. Finished golden or fumed.

No. 1 black leather........................	$12.50
Spanish leather...........................	12.50
Mole skin.................................	11.50

IMPORTANT—Be sure to specify finish of Woodwork desired, also whether Black or Brown Spanish Leather. No. 1 Leather is always furnished unless otherwise ordered.

Janney, Semple, Hill & Co. Minneapolis.

No. 21071—MISSION MORRIS CHAIR

Selected quartersawed oak, any style of finish. Very massive. Loose cushions, filled with pure white cotton.

Boston leather, black or Spanish.......	$29.00
Mole skin, black or Spanish.............	32.00
No. 2 leather, black or Spanish........	39.00
No. 1 leather, black or Spanish........	48.00

No. 21685—MISSION MORRIS CHAIR

Size of post, 2¼ in.; arms, 3½ in.; 41 in. high. Quartersawed oak, any finish. Loose cushions filled with pure white cotton.

Boston leather........................	$23.00
Mole skin, black or Spanish............	24.00
No. 2 leather, black or Spanish.........	26.00
No. 1 guaranteed leather, black or Spanish	32.00

No. 21080—MISSION MORRIS CHAIR

Selected oak. Loose cushions.

Verona	$16.00
Boston leather, black or Spanish.......	17.00
Mole skin, black or Spanish............	19.00
No. 2 leather, black or Spanish........	27.50
No. 1 leather, black or Spanish........	36.00

IMPORTANT—Be sure to specify finish of Woodwork desired, also whether Black or Brown Spanish Leather. No. 1 Leather is always furnished unless otherwise ordered.

Janney, Semple, Hill & Co. Minneapolis.
209

No. 15702-6US—UPHOLSTERED ROCKER

Best spring construction. Finish, golden or fumed oak.

Price, dozen..........................$132.00

No. 16226-6MC—ROCKER

Quartered oak. Motor seat. Genuine leather. Finish, fumed or golden oak.

Price, each............................$10.00

15702-6US

16226—6MC

No. 15742-6MC—ROCKER

Quartered oak. Motor seat. Genuine leather. Either black or Spanish. Finish, fumed oak.

Price, each............................$15.00

No. 15927-6UB—ROCKER

Upholstered back and seat. Finish, fumed or golden oak.

Price, each............................$13.50

15742-6MC

15927-6UB

IMPORTANT—Be sure to specify finish of Woodwork desired.

Janney, Semple, Hill & Co. Minneapolis.
201

No. 21684½—ROCKER

Quartersawed oak. 2-in. post; 4-in. arm; 38 in. high. Finished fumed or golden oak. Pad back with a loose automobile cushion seat.

Mole skin, black or Spanish......$19.00

No. 2 leather, black or Spanish.... 20.50

No. 1 guaranteed leather, black or Spanish 24.00

No. 21670½—MISSION ROCKER

Quartersawed oak, finished fumed or golden oak. 2½-in. posts; 5-in. arms; 36 in. high.

Mole skin, black or Spanish............... $23.00

No. 2 leather, black or Spanish............... 24.00

No. 1 guaranteed leather, black or Spanish... 27.00

Arm chair to match.

No. 21671½—AUTO SEAT ROCKER

Quartersawed oak. Finished fumed or golden oak. 2½-in. posts; 5-in. arms; 37 in. high. Upholstered back with loose automobile cushion seat.

Mole skin, black or Spanish.................$25.00

No. 2 leather, black or Spanish.............. 27.50

No. 1 guaranteed leather, black or Spanish.. 31.00

IMPORTANT—Be sure to specify finish of Woodwork desired, also whether Black or Brown Spanish Leather. No. 1 Leather is always furnished unless otherwise ordered.

The following pages contain advertisements that appeared in 1911 and 1913 issues of The Fra, a magazine of the "American philosophy" that included articles on topics ranging from women's suffrage to social conditions in the United States. It was published by Elbert Hubbard, who founded the Roycroft Arts and Crafts Community in East Aurora, N.Y., in 1895.

THE ROYCROFT CONVENTION

THE Sixteenth Annual Convention will be held at East Aurora, July First to Tenth, inclusive, Nineteen Hundred Eleven.

All Life Members, and subscribers to *The Fra* and *The Philistine* in good standing, are especially invited to be with us and join in the gladsome glee. ¶ There will be two formal programs daily, but not too formal—afternoon and evening—when men and women of note will speak, sing, recite, vibrate and otherwise disturb the ether.

There is always much good-fellowship at these conventions. Introductions are tabu. Everybody knows everybody else. Good will and the laugh in which there is no bitterness prevail.

¶ The Science of Business, this year, will be one of the especial themes under discussion.

Music will be a principal feature.

The Roycroft Physical Director will lead gentle walks afield —down to the Spring and through The Roycroft Wood. There will also be tramps to The Roycroft Farm—there usually are—and demonstrations at The Roycroft Woodpile.

Health, happiness, good cheer and all that makes for increased efficiency will be yours.

As for Ideas, everybody is welcome to all he can bring, and to all he can carry away.

There is no charge for attendance at the lectures, concerts and other entertainments.

Rates at The Roycroft Inn are Two Dollars a day and up, according to rooms, including meals.

Free automobile service meets all trains at the station. Reservations at the Inn can now be made. Perhaps you had better not dress too fine—flannels, corduroys, khaki, stout shoes and a smile!

THE ROYCROFT INN, EAST AURORA, NEW YORK

The Roycroft School of Life for Boys opens September 10th. Write to The Roycrofters for catalog.

ENTRANCE · TO · THE · ROYCROFT · INN

The Roycroft Inn

THE Roycroft Inn is a hotel—American plan—but it is something else beside.

It is a symphony in tints and tones, and a study in the grain of woods. The buildings that make The Roycroft Inn were built by The Roycrofters; the furniture was thought out by the same heads and made by the same hands that built The Inn.

You can forget the woes that you've been manufacturing all Winter, at The Roycroft.

There is a cool restiness about the long Peristyle by the fountain that sends weary city days into the limbo of distance.

There are cattle on our thousand hills and woods and meadowland, all the wholesome things of country life, and right at the heart of it, a world industry.

The Roycroft Shops are open at all times to our guests. This is the sixteenth year of their development.

So every Summer there are some who journey Roycroft-way by the Twentieth Century or Pierce-Arrow routes.

June is the month of commencements, marital commencements, and the like. Brides, grooms, sweet girl graduates and their fond parents—and those workaday bodies who need a brief rebuilding spell—are welcomed, made at home and left to their own sweet devices.

We serve simple, wholesome, well-prepared food produced on The Roycroft Farm, at Round Tables that would have charmed King Arthur's Knights.

We pass the medicine-ball and exclude the bilious bolus dupe and dope ❧ We gather at the pump, refresh ourselves at the eternal spring, and follow the good dictum of early to bed and early to rise.

❡ All themes are discussed save your troubles and your ills.

The Roycrofters are healthy, reasonably wealthy, happy and fairly wise. They send you greeting and welcome to The Roycroft Inn.

The rate for simple, well-ordered rooms is $2.00 and $2.50 a day.

❡ De-luxe suits with out-of-door sleeping-apartments, $3.00 a day.

❡ Choice suites, with sleeping-porches and bath, $4.00. Extra De-luxe rooms, $5.00 a day.

Good automobile roads from anywhere to everywhere connect with East Aurora and The Roycroft Inn.

❡ All kinds of benzine-buggies, including Uncle Hiram's chug-chug.

THE ROYCROFT INN
East Aurora, New York State

The Roycroft School of Life for Boys opens September 10th. Write to The Roycrofters for catalog.

BANKING BY MAIL

THE idea suggested itself one day, when one of our boys asked to have us hold back three dollars a week from his pay and give the accumulation to him January First. You see, he had a thrift bee in his bonnet and wanted us to help him help himself. Going to buy a lot and build a house on it!

Right there, it occurred to us that this was an opportunity for us to enlarge the idea and help all our people who were so inclined. So, under the title of Elbert Hubbard, Banker, we paved the way. Simply a scheme whereby the boys and girls could have banking facilities handy, and at the same time derive more benefits than banks usually offer. About three hundred Roycrofters have accounts with us now, and when one of them needs a little money to start a home with, why, he can have it. We do not loan money to outsiders, and, in fact, do not want outsiders' business. The policy of the concern is a conservative one, and the main object a lesson — education and opportunity. ¶We can just as well handle two or three hundred more accounts with the same expense, and so Roycrofters-at-Large are offered our banking opportunities. ¶All accounts are subject to check at any time: we pay Four per cent interest per annum on quarterly balances, computed and added to the account quarterly. Deposits of One Dollar and up received. ¶East Aurora is a safe place to put that accumulating account for your boy and girl (and yourself, too).

ELBERT HUBBARD, *Banker*

EAST AURORA, ERIE COUNTY, NEW YORK

The Roycroft School of Life for Boys opens September 10th. Write to The Roycrofters for catalog.

Pillows and Table Covers That Have Individuality

The Roycroft stock of leather is selected by men who know leather values.

Some extra special skins are put by for table covers and spreads for people of discrimination.

Pillows and spreads of the same color-tone give a cozy touch to your room scheme. These Roycroft furnishings are distinctive, they have personality, and they add an air of fitness wherever they are used.

We have these skins in brown, blue, green, gray and red.

PILLOWS

The full skin pillows are 20 by 20 inches in all colors, $5.00.

We make a special plain skin pillow with laced edges 20 by 20 inches, $6.00.

TABLE-COVERS

Velvet sheepskins in all colors, $2.00.

Goatskins, each, $3.00.

Very fine quality calfskins, each, $4.00.

THE ROYCROFTERS, EAST AURORA, ERIE COUNTY, NEW YORK

The Roycroft School of Life for Boys opens September 10th. Write to The Roycrofters for catalog.

HISTORY & ROMANCE IN FURNITURE
A Retrospect by Elbert Hubbard

THE history of a people is commonly figured forth in its furniture. ¶ The things we make show to the world what we are. ¶ The Furniture of a period is a sure index to the ideals and aspirations of that period—or to the lack of them. ¶ And right here is a good place to observe that History is divided and subdivided into Periods, for the most part distinctly differentiated. ¶ We have the Age of Pericles in Athens, a time when the Greek genius attained the top notch of brilliancy and grandeur.

Under the leadership of Pericles, the arts flourished and Athens was unquestionably the capital of the world, from the standpoint of artistic and literary achievement.

"The glory that was Greece" was never more glorious than during this brief period of Periclean-Athenian ascendency.

The Greeks had little furniture in their homes, and that little was fashioned mostly after Oriental models.

The Greeks were an outdoor people, like the Greeks of our own day.

And for folk who lead the simple life out of doors, a very few household articles suffice.

Not until the time of the Renaissance did furniture begin to take on modern characteristics. With the advent of the New Birth, the medieval mind experienced a quickening process that shadowed forth the dawning of a new and better day.

The pent-up genius of the Middle Ages burst forth in a flood of fine furniture ✒ The Renaissance brought in new ways of thinking, and this "new thought" was applied not merely to religion and literature and politics, but to dress, furniture and household furnishings, as well.

The growth of sedentary habits, unknown to the Ancients and the people of the Middle Ages, inaugurated a new regime, and the development of furniture was largely dependent on this change in ways of living.

From being sparse, splendid, massive, costly, furniture became plentiful, inferior in quality, light, cheap.

The cabinetmaker's art reached its culmination in the Eighteenth Century ✒ This was the great furniture period in every European country. Originality and initiative waxed brilliant, and the designs wrought out by the master craftsmen of England, France, Germany and Holland have never been surpassed. The best we can do today is to make impressive replicas of these masterpieces.

The originals are mostly worth many times their weight in gold; but for a song, comparatively, we can today revel in the bold and pleasing conceptions of such artisans as Chippendale, Sheraton, Heppel-White, Shearer, the Adam Brothers, and others composing the Eighteenth-Century School of Cabinetmakers in Merrie England.

Berkey and Gay have spent their lives in the endeavor to reproduce the designs of these masters. ¶ There are more than four thousand separate pieces of this Berkey and Gay Furniture, any one of them worth more to the thinking man or woman than a whole houseful of the ordinary and nondescript stuff that by the grace of nobody in particular masquerades under the name of "furniture." ¶ Berkey and Gay are pioneers in the production of Period Furniture that will rival comparison with the originals themselves.

The next best thing to owning one of these priceless originals is to buy a Berkey and Gay.

Berkey and Gay have succeeded in capturing the thought and the ideals expressed in the originals and imprisoning them in the reproductions.

Berkey and Gay Furniture will last longer, look better and yield more genuine satisfaction than a carload of the stuff with which the generality of people disgrace their domiciles.

Write for the exquisite Berkey and Gay brochure, *Character in Furniture*, illustrated by the French artist, Rene Vincent. It is yours for just fifteen two-cent stamps. Be sure to ask for a copy of Eugene Field's amusing ditty, entitled, *In Amsterdam*. Field was an ardent admirer of Berkey and Gay Furniture. He voices his enthusiasm in this characteristic rhyme.

This shopmark on every piece of Berkey and Gay Furniture is a means of identification, and a protection to purchasers.

BERKEY AND GAY FURNITURE COMPANY
192 Monroe Avenue, Grand Rapids, Michigan

Modeled–Leather Mats

S lamp or vase mats on hall, den or library table, these exquisitely colored, superbly executed specimens of modeled-leather work are efficient and effective. They give an added touch of grace and dignity to your furnishings. ❈ Made in Ivy-Wreath, Thorn-Apple, Lotus, Mistletoe, Rose, Moth and Dragon-Fly Designs, in the following sizes and at prices stated ❈ ❈ ❈ ❈ ❈ ❈ ❈ ❈ ❈

VASE-MATS

7 in. diam.	$1.00
8 " "	1.25
9 " "	1.50
10 " "	1.75

LAMP-MATS

12 in. diam.	$2.25
15 " "	3.50
18 " "	5.00
20 " "	7.50
22 " "	10.00

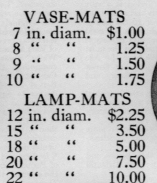

ROSE DESIGN
15 inches diameter
Price, $3.50

MISTLETOE DESIGN
15 inches diameter
Price, $3.50

CONVENTIONAL ROSE DESIGN
18 inches diameter
Price, $5.00

The Roycrofters, East Aurora, New York

"Let us to Billiards!"—*Shakespeare*

Being a Few Remarks by Fra Elbertus on a "most gentle, cleanly and ingenious game."

CHARLES COTTON, the friend of Izaak Walton, published, in Sixteen Hundred Seventy-Four, a book which he called *The Compleat Gamester*.

It was modeled after Walton's best-known work, even as to title, and served as a sort of guide to the popular pastimes of the day.

"King" Cotton's work was an authority. Instead of quoting "Hoyle," folks of that time did things "according to Cotton."

Billiards was in as high repute in England two centuries and a half ago as it is today, according to the testimony of this man Cotton, who writes in part: "For the excellency of the recreation, it is much approved of and played by most nations of Europe, especially in England, there being few towns of note therein which hath not a public billiard-table—neither are they wanting in many noble and private families in the country."

This might have been written yesterday in point of applicability.

Billiards has been called "the gentleman's game." It has ever appealed to the true sportsman, for there is probably no game played today in which the element of chance is a less important factor. Skill is the mainspring, and skill can be developed only by constant and consistent application. A billiard-table in the home is worth two in the down-town district. For, cynical remarks "to the contrary notwithstanding," as they say in the novels, home is the best place for girl or boy, man or maid, and for their parents and grand-parents, as well.

"There's no place like home," said John Howard Payne, the man who had none, and then added significantly, "especially if there's a Brunswick-Balke-Collender Billiard-Table in it!"

There is really only one concern in the billiard business today—the Brunswick-Balke-Collender Company. More than eighty per cent of the billiard-tables now in use were ushered into existence by this firm.

The firstlings of this flock have been adopted into the best families with a readiness that is not a bit surprising when you know the truth.

The Brunswick "Baby Grand" Billiard-Table has introduced the good old scientific game of billiards into hundreds of homes.

It is made in Mahogany, with inlaid design—genuine Vermont slate bed, imported billiard-cloth—standard quick-action Baby Monarch cushions. Concealed Cue-Rack and accessory drawer holds entire playing equipment. The Brunswick "Convertible" Billiard-Table can be metamorphosed into a dining or library table or davenport, when not in use in its normal capacity.

❦ Send for color booklet, *The Home Magnet*—and to that end just fill in the blank below.

The Brunswick-Balke-Collender Co.,   Dept. G U, 623-633 *S. Wabash Avenue, Chicago, U. S. A.*

Gentlemen: Please send to the address below your Easy Purchase Proposition and Book—*BILLIARDS—THE HOME MAGNET.*

Name...

Street..

Town.................State......................

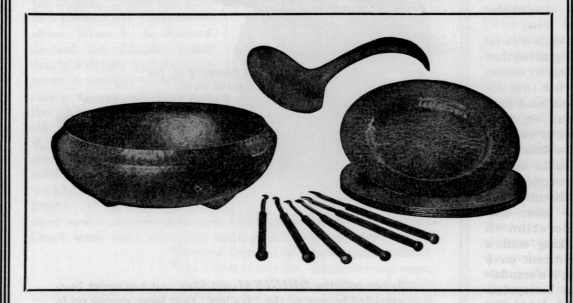

Globe-Wernicke

Filing Equipment

MOST mistakes that occur in filing and finding papers would be avoided if you had a Globe-Wernicke Filing Cabinet. ¶ Filing, even in the hands of the irrepressible office boy — with his heart at the World's Series, and his eyes and ears alert for the " Wuxtry ! "— is a safe and reliable proposition, when he uses the mechanically perfect and automatically faultless

Globe-Wernicke
Safeguard System

Globe-Wernicke Filing Cabinets represent modern filing efficiency. They are built on G / W Sectional principles which provide for the expansion of business. They are made in all styles, finishes and sizes, and equipped with units and compartments to accommodate the peculiarities of any office. ¶ Our local Agent will be glad to demonstrate the advantages and economy of Globe-Wernicke aids to better office system. Where not represented we ship freight prepaid. Send to us for Booklet No. 12, on Office and Filing Equipment.

The Globe-Wernicke Co.

Makers of Sectional Bookcases, Filing Cabinets and Supplies

FACTORY, CINCINNATI

TO CONVINCE YOU

THAT ROYCROFT
FURNITURE IS ALL WE CLAIM FOR IT,
THIS OFFER IS MADE

HERE is one of our most popular pieces — a combination reading-table and bookshelves — the regular price of which is Fifteen Dollars F. O. B. East Aurora, N. Y. Just as long as the orders keep coming, we will send one of these pieces anywhere in the United States, East of the Mississippi, freight prepaid, for the one sum of Twelve Dollars, cash with order. To Western points, we will prepay freight to the Mississippi, and you pay the rest.

Combination Reading-Table and Bookshelves, No. 022
Top, 15 x 26 inches ; Height, 30 inches

¶ Now this is not a "knock-down" offer, but is what most people know as a "leader." It is at one time a generous and a selfish proposition. You are offered a piece of furniture below its usual selling-price, and we sacrifice profits on it, hoping to interest you in further purchases of other pieces. Don't you see, we make this simple, substantial, straight-line furniture with our head, hand and heart. We believe that which serves best distracts least. Things in evidence must be unassuming and dignified. You can not afford to harass your nerves with gaudy and noisy surroundings. ¶ This particular piece of Roycroft Furniture will lend itself to the surroundings ; and no matter what the style is, there will be no clash. There is a quiet dignity about it that is well substantiated by its utility and capacity to serve. ¶ Just see for yourself how useful it may be — and it takes up very little room. ¶ We finish it in Roycroft Brown, a soft, deep shade that peculiarly brings out the beautiful grain of quartered oak. ¶ Your order will be filled promptly, on receipt. Write us about it today ✠ ✠ ✠ ✠

The Roycroft line of furniture includes a varied assortment of designs for Dining-Room, Den, Library and Bedroom in quartered oak or solid mahogany. Send twenty-five cents for a complete catalog.

THE ROYCROFT FURNITURE SHOP
EAST AURORA, NEW YORK

THE importance of Loyalty in Business could not readily be overestimated, even though its sole function were to secure united action on the part of the officers and men ✍ Where no two men or groups of men are working to counter purposes, but all are united in a common purpose, the gain would be enormous, even though the amount of energy put forth by the individuals was not increased in the least ✍ When to this fact of value in organized effort we add the accompanying psychological facts of increased Efficiency by means of Loyalty, we then begin to comprehend what it means to have or to lack Loyalty ✍

The employer who secures the Loyalty of his men not only secures better service, but he enables his men to accomplish with less effort and less exhaustion. The creator of Loyalty is a Public Benefactor.

Such Loyalty is always reciprocal. The feeling which workmen entertain for their employer is usually a reflection of his attitude towards them. Fair wages, reasonable hours, working quarters and conditions of average comfort and healthfulness, and a measure of protection against accident are no more than primary requirements in a factory or store. Without them, labor of the better, more energetic types can not be secured in the first place or held for any length of time. And the employer who expects, in return for these, any more than the average of uninspired service is sure to be disappointed.—*Walter Dill Scott.*

✍

The highest aim of all authority is to confer liberty.—*William E. Channing.*

Indirect Lighting Fixtures

No. X-55

SELECT lighting fixtures as you do heating devices, for efficiency as well as for looks. ¶ The usefulness of the charcoal-brazier and the coal-stove has passed away. In their time they were the best we had, but with them were disadvantages. This old method gave inefficient heating. Steam and hot water have supplanted it, because of their efficiency, convenience and beauty. ¶ Just as we want warmth, but not fire, so we need illumination, but not light. Glaring light, like an intensely hot fire, is a cause. Diffused illumination, like grateful warmth, is an effect. ¶ An object is well illuminated when it can be easily seen, without fatigue or eye-strain. You will readily recognize the requirements for comfort in lighting. There must be sufficient light by which to see easily, but not too much light. For its glare fatigues and produces a garish, unnatural atmosphere in the room. ¶ Harsh shadows should be absent, as they produce a disagreeable, unhygienic effect. ¶ We put the furnace in the cellar, out of sight, and now we are hiding the lights in opaque bowls, urns and pedestals — and so have evenly diffused their reflected rays to produce a gentle, uniform radiance throughout the room. ¶ This indirect illumination is free from glare and produces no eye-strain. It softens harsh shadows and illuminates rich appointments and fine architectural effects in an incomparable manner. In any corner of the room we may read, write or rest with comfort and pleasure. ¶ We may look directly at the lighting fixture and experience no discomfort. The furniture may be arranged without regard to where the light will fall. Glossy papers under this illumination will give back no irritating reflection. ¶ This is the "Eye-Comfort Lighting System." No more appropriate name exists. It is the rational illumination for all time. Its success attests this fact. We all are interested in this lighting for some interior — home, church, hotel, office, bank or theater. ¶ Ask us to forward the booklet describing and picturing what has been accomplished in lighting effects for the particular kind of interior in which you are interested. ¶ We want to bring this lighting system to your attention, and will gladly send full information about the Indirect Lighting Fixtures. Your asking for this implies no obligation on your part ᔰ ᔰ ᔰ ᔰ ᔰ ᔰ ᔰ ᔰ ᔰ

The Roycroft Shop
East Aurora, N. Y.

No. X-56

Hand-Hammered Copper Nut-Set

WORDSWORTH'S picture of himself as a boy on that heavenly day when, in the eagerness of boyish hope, he left the cottage threshold, sallying forth with a huge wallet slung over his shoulder, a nutting-crook in his hand, and turned his step toward a far distant wood, is a picture of many another boy in many another land in nutting season. ¶Spring and fishing, Fall and nutting—these are the common seasons and the common joys of boyhood. The boy gets his whole pleasure when he brings home the "wallet" filled with brown, shiny treasure. ¶For him a flat stone in the woodshed and a hammer is a nut service fit for a king. ¶This hand-wrought copper nut-bowl with nut-plates, spoon and picks is for the boy's mother. With these she will rightly enjoy the season's Harvest.

Complete Set	-	-	-	-	-	-	-	-	$15.00
Nut-Bowl	-	-	-	-	-	-	-	-	6.00
Individual Plates, each	-	-	$ .75	Set	-	-	4.00
Nut-Picks, each	-	-	-	.75	Set	-	-	4.50
Service-Spoon	-	-	-	-	-	-	-	-	1.50

The Roycrofters, East Aurora, Erie Co., New York

Ooze-Leather
Table-Covers and Pillows

Ooze-leather table-covers and pillows in the same color-tone are especially suitable and pleasing for use in libraries and dens. They help to make harmony and hominess.

PILLOWS

Whole-skin pillows, 20 x 20 inches, all colors. Price, Five Dollars.

Plain skin pillows with laced edges, 20 x 20 inches, all colors. Price, Six Dollars.

TABLE-COVERS

Velvet-finish sheepskins in brown, green, gray, red, tan. Price, Two Dollars.

Goatskins, selected colors. Price, Three Dollars.

Very fine quality calfskins, selected colors. Price, Four Dollars.

The Roycrofters, East Aurora, N.Y.

Modeled-Leather Screen

Designed by Frederick C. Kranz

There is only one screen like this. There will be no other. The dining-room that will own this one as part of its beauty will have a marked place in the memory of every one who sees it. Price, Two Hundred Dollars.

Modeled-Leather Wastebasket

A Wastebasket is a necessity in every library, office and den, if you value the Axminster or your hardwood floors. But a wastebasket with too much ego offends the poetic unities.

This modeled-leather basket never lops, leaks nor lapses. It is dignified, poised, quiet and rarely beautiful.

The design and workmanship are distinctly Roycroft Standard.

Why not make yourself a present? The price is $10.00.

THE ROYCROFTERS

EAST AURORA, ERIE COUNTY, NEW YORK

9 inches diameter by 15 inches deep

No Enemy But Himself

A Novel by Elbert Hubbara

THERE are just twenty-six copies of *No Enemy but Him-
self* left from the last edition
printed at the Knickerbocker
Press in Nineteen Hundred Seven.

These books will interest collectors
of Elbert Hubbard's writings, because
they are offered here for the last time.

No Enemy but Himself is the story of
a life—lived foolishly, perhaps, but
intensely lived to the strange end of it.

In gray cloth binding, Price, $1.25

THE ROYCROFTERS
East Aurora New York

DON'T be a Christmas
Rusher, and get red in the
face. Order your Roycroft
Wares early and save your time
and temper ✒ You know what
those last few days before
Christmas are — BE WISE!

SIX DE-LUXE DOLLAR BOOKS

 ONE-DOLLAR Roycroft book has several distinctive qualities
that make it individual and unforgetable.

¶ The ooze-leather binding, the lining of silk to harmonize with
the cover, the quality of the handmade imported paper—all
these things make up what is recognized as Roycroft Quality.

¶ The books listed here are the few scattered volumes left from editions that
are all but sold out. Books that will not be reprinted, and that have the charm
and lure of being First Editions.

CHICAGO TONGUE
by Elbert Hubbard
¶ A preachment on the subject of the unruly
member.

ADDISON
by Elbert Hubbard
¶ A Little Journey to the home of that gentle genius
whose "Spectator" was the first real daily paper
ever published.

THE BASIS OF MARRIAGE
by Alice Hubbard
¶ A reasonable treatise on the unreasonable.

BOTTICELLI
by Elbert Hubbard
¶ A Little Journey to the home of a great Colorist.

BRAHMS
by Elbert Hubbard
¶ The story of a maker of great Music.

COMTE
by Elbert Hubbard
¶ A Little Journey to the home of a thinker, and
incidentally some bits of philosophy.

These books are done in ooze binding, silk-lined, silk marker. Special titles and initials.   Price of each, $1.00.

THE ROYCROFTERS, EAST AURORA, NEW YORK

A Workbasket

Alice Carey, in her "Pictures That Hang on Memory's Wall," gives us all a little thrill of recollection. We see with her the picture that we love best of all—perhaps not the same picture, but one that is simple and close to our childhood.

The workbasket, piled high with every size of stockings, that was always on mother's table by the window, just where she could look out and see us at our play, is a vivid picture for some of us.

The Roycrofters have made some Leather Workbaskets, with a soft velvet-leather lining, that will delight every woman. We have them in Ecru, Gray, Green, Brown, Tan, Old Rose and Maroon. They are 3 1-2 x 9 inches. Price, $1.50.

THE ROYCROFTERS, EAST AURORA, ERIE CO., NEW YORK

GOLD has been used as the medium for color harmony ever since the blending of shades and tones was recognized as a fine art.

¶ Here we have the reason for the gold threads used in tapestries; for the cloth-of-gold background in rare embroideries, and gold as the setting for gems.

¶ Roycroft Modeled-Leather Mats possess a unique, distinctive harmony of color-tone because the art shades used are softened and blended with gold.

¶ Two or three mats of different sizes can be used to advantage on your library-table.

TABLE-MATS—various designs—
18 inches in diameter $5.00
LAMP-MATS—
12 inches in diameter 2.25
VASE-MATS—
8 inches in diameter 1.25

The Roycrofters :: East Aurora :: New York

What are you going to do with that boy of yours? Write us for information regarding The Roycroft School.

The Age of Big Business

THIS is the Age of Big Business. Maurice Maeterlinck tells us that a bee alone has no intelligence and away from the hive it is lost and undone. So it is with men. We are interdependent and only as we co-operate do we do big and worthy things.

Organization is the keynote of success ✒ System is the twin of organization. George H. Burr and Company, Bankers, are assisting people to enjoy the benefits of the Age of Big Business, by offering carefully selected industrial stocks of true merit and security to the average man who from his savings has the necessary capital to participate.

The securities offered by this reliable Banking Concern are seasoned and substantial, and bring a reasonable yield of profit ✒ Marketable securities of absolutely safe quality are the only ones which interest Messrs. Burr and Company. They believe that wealth should be used for human good, and being wise they know that this is the best business policy.

Their list of the Industrial Preferred Stocks is practically a list of Class A enterprises of America. The endeavor is to interest the intelligent and industrious American to invest only in the highest-class securities, bonds and preferred stocks.

What the world needs is more wealth and a wider distribution of it. And to share in the profits of such concerns as those listed below recommended for investment by George H. Burr and Company is both desirable and right: American Car and Foundry Company, American Piano Company, American Radiator Company, American Sugar Refining Company, American Woolen Company, Brunswick-Balke-Collender Company, General Chemical Company, International Harvester Company, McCrum-Howell Company, National Biscuit Company.

Definite details in regard to Industrial Preferred Shares will be gladly sent on request. Any information regarding investments which are referred to this Company will receive thoughtful and faithful attention.

George H. Burr & Company, Bankers

37 Wall Street .:. New York City

A Good Value

Cadillac "Desk-Table"

❧ If the Cadillac Desk-Table were offered a few years ago, it would be at a price which would make it accessible to only the "favored few" who possess wealth. ❧ Modern methods of manufacture and distribution have made it possible to offer these wonderful tables at a price which will not be a burden to very many people.

❧ The Wolverine Manufacturing Company are the largest manufacturers of Parlor and Library tables in the world. Their output is a "table a minute," which explains the very low price at which this desk-table is now offered.

No. 236

Table Number 236, here illustrated, can be bought for $10.50 at any Furniture-Store East of the Mississippi and North of the Ohio Rivers.

❧ Simply pulling open a drawer provides desk space with non-spillable inkwell and pen-groove, with large roomy drawer beneath desk-lid for stationery and correspondence. Nothing on the table needs to be disturbed.

❧ Choice of seventy-five designs, at prices to suit in every style, covered by four patents.

❧ Styles include reproductions of "Period Furniture," Louis XIV, Elizabethan, Tudor, Flanders, Colonial, Arts and Crafts and Modern Designs; made by skilled craftsmen from the finest materials obtainable.

❧ Look for the patented easy-sliding, nickel-plated steel slide, which allows the drawer to open freely. Counterbalanced to prevent tipping.

Booklet "B" showing our complete line in half-tone pictures will be mailed upon request.

No. 267

Wolverine Mfg. Co., Detroit, Mich.:

Gentlemen—Please send me your booklet "B" free.

My Name _____

My Address _____

My Dealer is _____

THE man who lacks faith in other men loses his best chances to work, and gradually undermines his own power and his own character. We do not realize to what extent others judge us by our beliefs ❧ But we are in fact judged in that way; and it is right that we should be judged in that way. The man who is cynical, whether about women or business or politics, is assumed (and in nineteen cases out of twenty, with full justice) to be immoral in his relations to women or business or politics. The man who has faith in the integrity of others in the face of irresponsible accusations is assumed (and in nineteen

cases out of twenty, justly assumed) to have the confidence in others' goodness because he is a good man himself.—*President Hadley.*

❧

BROWNING is almost alone in the peculiar height and delicacy of his interpretation of womanhood, and Pompilia is the crowning illustration of this.

She is the heroic type of womanhood, rising in perfect response to every height of experience, discerning through utter sincerity and transparency of soul the truth in the highest relations of human life.

There is infinite delicacy and yet depths in Browning's reading of the secrets of the woman's soul, the glory and beauty of her motherhood. Pompilia is even nearer than Caponsacchi to The Truth ❧ In each the supreme hunger is to serve the good of the other, infinitely and forever, rather than to be made happy by or to be loved and satisfied. —*Edward Howard Griggs.*

A Stein Song

> For it's always fair weather,
> When good fellows get together,
> With a stein on the table and a good song ringing clear.

Richard Hovey and Bliss Carmen were prince-rovers and Kings of Vagabondia. ¶ Together these true comrades found the joys of the open road, and all the wholesome, friendly, natural things that belong to a natural way of living. They were merry souls, these two, and their verses are filled with the lure, lilt and laughter that was in their hearts. The Stein Song is a joyous echo of some happy day when Richard Hovey sang out:

> For we're all frank-and-twenty,
> When Spring is in the air,
> And we've faith and hope a-plenty,
> And we've life and love to spare.

The Roycroft Stein is made from hand-hammered copper, with sterling-silver trimmings and handle. The cover and top band are set with jade. The lining is silver-plated. ¶ Height, six inches; diameter, four and one-half inches. Price, $25.00. ¶ The Roycroft Steins are specially made. Get in your Christmas Order now.

The Roycrofters, East Aurora, Erie County, New York

What are you going to do with that boy of yours? Write us for information regarding The Roycroft School.

A study in oak from Charles the First period

Berkey & Gay Signed Furniture

An Advertisement by Elbert Hubbard

Human imagination can not conceive of how Turner's work could be improved upon.—*John Ruskin.*

THERE are some things the world can not improve upon. They are just as good as they can be, and any attempt to make them better is time wasted. ❡ Imagine, for instance, perfecting the Hermes of Praxiteles!—or beating old blind Homer at his own little game of dictating epics!—or inventing color-schemes superior to those that Titian lavished on his immortal canvases!

To extend the analogy, imagine attempting to construct better furniture than that built by Berkey & Gay! ❡ It is good to gain perfection; but perfection once gained, discretion is the part of wisdom.

For more than half a hundred years Berkey & Gay have been making furniture that is a source of joy and infinite satisfaction.

Berkey & Gay are specialists in Period Furniture. Whether your taste inclines to the highly ornate, decorative styles of Louis XV, or to the simple, massive lines of the Colonial Period, you can find what you are looking for, in pieces of Berkey & Gay make. ❡ Berkey & Gay have rendered our times an undoubted service by adapting for use in Twentieth-Century homes, all the famous patterns which we associate with the names of Sheraton, Chippendale, the Adam brothers, William and Mary, Colonial, and so forth.

Berkey & Gay furniture is made honestly and well. " Quality goes in before the price goes on." Workmanship is the prime factor—the price a secondary consideration. ❡ Berkey & Gay sign their furniture, just as an author signs his book or a painter his canvas. The Berkey & Gay Shopmark is inlaid in every piece of Berkey & Gay furniture. It is a hallmark of identification, indicating the makers' supreme confidence in the quality of their product.

Berkey & Gay do not issue a catalog. Their furniture is not of that ilk. Your dealer, however, will show you a magnificent Art Portfolio of Direct Photogravures picturing each of more than two thousand pieces of Berkey & Gay furniture, from which choice may be made. If you do not know who the dealer in your locality is, Berkey & Gay will tell you. ❡ Meanwhile, send fifteen two-cent United States stamps for the de-luxe booklet, *Character in Furniture,* which explains the history and significance of Period Furniture. It is beautifully illustrated by Rene Vincent, the French artist, who has caught the spirit of Berkey & Gay furniture, and imparted it to these original drawings. ❡ Ask also for a copy of Eugene Field's humorous "Pome," *In Amsterdam,* wherein mention is made of Berkey & Gay Furniture.

This is the inlaid mark of honor that is in and on every Berkey & Gay piece

Berkey & Gay Furniture Company
192 Monroe Avenue   **Grand Rapids, Michigan**

Why not mention THE FRA when writing to advertisers?

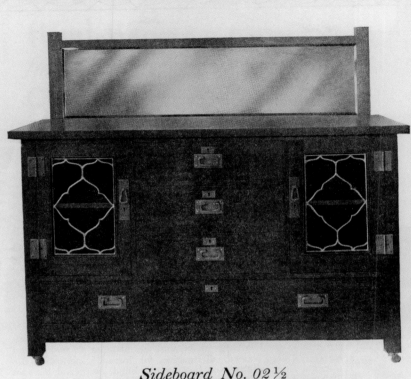

Sideboard No. 02½

60 *inches wide*   25 *inches deep*   38 *inches high*
14-*inch plate-glass mirror*
OAK, $85.00 ; MAHOGANY, $105.00
Coppered glass panels in doors, and handmade
copper trim throughout

F. O. B. East Aurora, N. Y.

YOUR DINING-ROOM ROYCROFTIE

WOULD give you the satisfaction and joy that one gets through having the thing just right. ¶ There is a dignified simplicity about Roycroft Furniture that lends an atmosphere of peace. The character of the workmanship and the finish at once impress you with their genuineness.

Our furniture is made by hand, every care being taken to make it as well as it can be done. Our ideals are set high and to a great degree have we realized them. When we learn how to make the furniture better, we will do it. ¶ Fix this in your mind : We make furniture for any place furniture may be used—the Library, Den, Dining-Room, Hall or Bedroom.

If you really care to know more about this furniture, send us 25 cents for a copy of our new complete catalog. There are a great many pieces illustrated in it that will be of much interest to you. An odd piece will fit in anywhere, if your needs do not require a whole set.

THE ROYCROFTERS
EAST AURORA, N.Y.

Send 25c for our new complete catalog, and pick out, say, a table, six chairs and a sideboard or china cabinet for that dining-room.

We teach boys to work—The Roycroft School for Boys at East Aurora, N. Y. Write for catalog.

THE DELIVERY CAR OF THE PRESENT

JUST as the horse superseded the ox, so is the International Commercial car taking the place of the horse in the world of business. There is no fairness to the ox or justice to the horse in comparing horses with oxen as workers. For the same reasons there is no comparison to be made between this good motor car and horses. From every point of view, except that of sentiment, the machine is superior.

How the International Commercial Car Works for You

¶ It does more work in less time. It travels faster. It works at the same speed all the time. It requires less care and no sympathy. It cannot get sick. It cannot die. As its parts wear out they can be replaced and the car kept constantly in working order. It effects a saving of time, money, and labor in every business where it can be kept busy. It increases the business territory of the man who uses it, and so makes more work for itself and more money for its owner. ¶ Built for commercial work, the International Commercial car delivers the goods, both literally and figuratively. It is made in two styles — air- and water- cooled ∙∙ Any special type of body desired can be fitted on the chassis. ¶ There is more than one pleasant surprise in store for the man who buys an International Commercial car. To find out all about the car, its capacity and its record, address

International Harvester
Company of America

(Incorporated)

160 Harvester Bldg., Chicago, U S A

HERE IS A BOOKCASE

No. 087 ½

32½ inches wide, 15½ inches deep, 39 inches high.
Oak, $16.00.
F. O. B. East Aurora, N. Y.

that will just take care of those few books and magazines that are always knocking around on top of the library-table — but which must be within sight and easy range. ¶Very substantially made, mortised and pinned, best quartered oak and Roycroft dull weathered finish. ¶ You need this in your library — and we can fill your order on receipt ❧ ❧ ❧ ❧ ❧ ❧ ❧

THE
ROYCROFTERS
Furniture-Shop
East Aurora, N. Y.

AN AMERICAN BIBLE — A Good Book to Start the Year With

To Those Who Stammer

MR. JOSEPH J. LAMB, of the Lamb School for Stammerers, knows everything about Stammering that will not work, and a goodly number of things that will. If you believe perfect speech essential to success, send for his catalogue, Gratis. It contains much useful information. His address is

**1252 Franklin Street
N. S., Pittsburgh, Pennsylvania**

Elbert Hubbard
𝔅𝔞𝔫𝔨𝔢𝔯
East Aurora, N. Y.

□□□

*You are invited to open
an account*

4% Interest Per Annum
figured and added to the account
Quarterly

□□□

*All accounts are subject
to check at any time*

Ask me about my interest-bearing Certificate of
Deposit for quiet accounts

Our sausage is **really** made on a farm. If we called it "Broadway Sausage" or "Chicago Sausage," any discriminating person who tasted it would know that it was made on a farm just the same.

JONES
❧ DAIRY FARM ❧
SAUSAGE

It is made in an old-fashioned way. Some folks would tell us we were wasteful of material, but we have never changed our opinion as to what to put into our sausage and what to leave out.

Young, milk-fed pork, pure spices, ground here at home, and salt are all the materials we have used or ever will use in sausage making.

We make fresh shipments to our regular grocers twice a week and sometimes oftener. All orders are made up and shipped the same day they are received. If you ask your grocer to take a "standing order," he will deliver you fresh sausage on the very days you want it. ¶ If your grocer cannot supply you, we will express sausage direct anywhere in U. S. or Canada. ¶ We will gladly give you more information about our farm products if you ask for it.

MILO C. JONES
Jones Dairy Farm
Box 622, Fort Atkinson, Wis.

The Farm

Suggestions for Valentine Gifts in Hand-Wrought Copper

Desk-Pad

Colonial Candlestick

Price, $2.00

Plain Copper Corners, size 16 x 22¾ inches
Price, $5.00
Copper Corners, Poppy design, 19 x 24 inches
Price, $7.00

Scimiter Paper-Knife

Price, 50 cents

Book-Ends

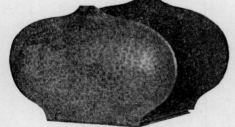

For Pocket Editions
Price, $2.00

Violet-Bowl

Price, $2.00

The Roycroft Shop, East Aurora, N. Y.

Eight men and one woman wrote this American Bible. Its publication marks an epoch.—FREDERICK D. UNDERWOOD.

Valentine Gifts for College Girls

It is a long wait from Christmas Holidays to Spring Vacation. To break this pleasantly, send a Valentine Box to the girl away at school. Here are a few suggestions for the box :

CHANGE-PURSE

Price, $2.00
One gusset pocket
One flat pocket

HAND-WROUGHT COPPER BOWL

Diameter, 6½ inches
Height, 3 inches
Price, $2.50

FULL-SKIN PILLOWS

Colors : Brown, green, gray and red
Price, $5.00
Sheepskin table-covers to match
$2.00 each

THE RUBAIYAT

A new pocket edition
Modeled-leather design
Price, $1.00

MODELED-LEATHER PHOTO-CASE

Size, 3 x 4½ inches
Two openings, square or oval
Price, $1.50

The Roycrofters, East Aurora, New York

An Epoch-Making Book—AN AMERICAN BIBLE.

What
ELBERT HUBBARD
thinks of
HENRY FORD

HENRY FORD, inventor and manufacturer of the Ford automobile, always reminds me of Thomas Jefferson. ¶ Ford is active, earnest, intelligent, sympathetic, courteous, kind. He is always well—always at work. He has the ability to co-operate with a vast number of people. He is a wise, able and safe leader. He is a teacher, and a teacher of teachers. Instinctively he is a farmer, a lover of the great Out-of-Doors, and is on good terms with himself. ¶ Henry Ford is a great Public Servant. ¶ With it all he has the far-reaching persistency and the honesty and the impelling love of truth that mark the extraordinary individual. In the office of the Ford Motor Company I saw an autographed picture of Thomas Edison, and below were the words — written in that unmistakable hand of the telegraph-operator, who prides himself on legibility:

To Henry Ford — one of a group of men who have helped to make the U. S. A. the most progressive Nation in the world.
— *Thomas A. Edison.*

¶ Henry Ford is as fine and as gentle as Luther Burbank, and is just as devoted. He is very seldom in the limelight and then not of his own choosing. He is a mechanic, an inventor, a naturalist. He loves the woods and the fields. He likes to work in his garden. He knows Nature in every form. But he also knows every part of his great and almost faultless manufacturing establishment. He moves among the men as one of them. They know him and respect him. ¶ Also, he respects them. ¶ He has time for a nod and a smile, and a word of greeting as he passes. ¶ Henry Ford has the ability to concentrate and consecrate. He is the only automobile-manufacturer today who invented his car, developed it in every part, and grew as his business grew. ¶ I regard it as one of the great privileges of my life to know Henry Ford. ¶ The successful man now is always a builder—he is always and forever widening, extending, expanding, improving, and it is all in the line of human service, and of human betterment. ¶ To exploit humanity is to fail, and all wise, successful men know it. ¶ To plunder is to die. ¶ Thomas Jefferson said that, through invention, creation, distribution and universal education, the United States would take a foremost place among the nations in the onward march of civilization. And the prophecy is coming true. ¶ As an inventor, creator, manufacturer, humanitarian, and public servant, the name of Henry Ford will endure. He will live in history, not only as one of the Makers of America, but as the one man who made it possible for all humanity to ride in motor-cars. ¶ The motto of Henry Ford is, "This one thing I do." ¶ He has standardized automobile-making until he has not a single competitor. He sells more machines, has more machines in process, has more raw stock on hand, and has more cash in the bank, than any other individual or automobile company in the world.

Elbert Hubbard

What
HENRY FORD
thinks of
THE "TUEC"

HEN Mr. Ford wrote this letter, he did it after making a personal examination of our machine — in fact, taking two of his mechanics to the basement, tearing the machine to pieces, thoroughly examining the construction, putting the machine together again, attaching it up to the current and the piping system, and the machine has never been touched since that time, which was over a year ago

---

FORD MOTOR COMPANY
AUTOMOBILE MANUFACTURERS

DETROIT, U. S A., May 13, 1911

The United Electric Co.
Canton, Ohio

Gentlemen:—

I am certainly gratified at the efficiency shown by ''TUEC'' Vacuum Cleaning System recently installed in our Administration Building. By a careful mechanical examination, I found that the very satisfactory working of these machines was due largely to the simplicity of their construction.

Our Office Building is 300' long by 60' wide, two stories and basement, and the TUEC cleaners, which have been in operation since February last, running all night long, have certainly proven beyond question that they are not only essential for absolute cleanliness but, being designed and constructed on the ''unit'' plan, are simple, durable and economical in operation, and I take pleasure in recommending them.

Very truly yours

Henry Ford

HF HJM

¶ The TUEC is a permanent, perfect system for taking the dirt, dust and bacteria out of stores, factories, schools, churches, sleeping-cars, day coaches — houses — at an insignificant cost. Write today for literature

The United Electric Company, Canton, Ohio.

COPPER PHOTOGRAPH-FRAMES

A PHOTOGRAPH-FRAME of hand-wrought copper is a new idea. The Roycrofters make a frame of simple and pleasing design. This frame is suitable for desk or dressing-table. It is four inches high and three and one-half inches wide. The price is One Dollar and Fifty Cents.

THE ROYCROFTERS, EAST AURORA, NEW YORK

MAKE YOUR OWN VALENTINES

YOU can decorate and make your own valentines, using the correspondence-cards which came in our recent importation of handmade stationery from Italy. So — your valentines will be characteristic and out of the ordinary. ¶ Both letter-paper and correspondence-cards will please people of discriminating tastes. The paper, cards and envelopes have the four deckle edges which distinguish handmade papers. The colors are green and brown in shades made only for The Roycrofters. ¶ The cards are three and three-fourths by six inches. ¶ The paper is six by seven and one-half inches. ¶ Price for cards or writing-paper, postpaid to any address, is One Dollar a box. ¶ We have a limited supply of Alexandra Vellum Letter-Paper, which sells at thirty-five cents a quire for paper and envelopes.

THE ROYCROFTERS, EAST AURORA, NEW YORK

FOUR GOSPELS

A FEW months ago we printed a book for Marilla Ricker, entitled, *The Four Gospels*. There are not many copies on hand at this time. ¶ Marilla Ricker is best known as the first woman to run for the office of Governor. She is a suffragist as the result of years of careful study of the question of " Woman's Rights." She is a deep, clear thinker, and her utterances are *worth considering*. ¶ The Four Gospels are entitled, Robert G. Ingersoll, Thomas Paine, John Calvin and Jonathan Edwards. ¶ There is an interesting Foreword by the author and a chapter headed, " What is Prayer." In the Foreword Mrs. Ricker says : " Youth believes that the world is eager for truth, and that every one wants the star of liberty to shine into his mind. Youth brings courage to the heart and joy to the world. The man who can carry the faith of youth through all the hard and dark ways of human life, still believing in the right, still speaking against the false and wrong, still urging truth against superstition and working to emancipate mankind, is a man to be applauded." ¶ The Price of the book is One Dollar.

THE ROYCROFTERS, EAST AURORA, NEW YORK

A PERPETUAL CALENDAR

Price, Two Dollars.

THIS is the month in which to change Calendars. Here is a new one made at The Roycroft Shops. The frame is of hand-wrought copper. The Calendar stands five inches high and is five and three-fourths inches wide. ¶ There are cards for each month and the days of the month. So, you have a calendar not for one year alone, but for all years. The cards are artistic and plainly printed. ¶ This Calendar will fit in nicely with your other desk accessories. ¶ The price is Two Dollars.

THE ROYCROFTERS, EAST AURORA, NEW YORK

We have a farm of 500 acres—also shops—where our boys learn to be self-respecting and self-supporting. The Roycroft School for Boys.